MORE PRAISE FOR

7 Keys to Comprehension

"7 *Keys to Comprehension* is a must read for all parents who are concerned about their children's reading. By following the authors' suggestions, your child will learn not only to read with confidence but love reading as well. It is a book that sets a new standard for how parents can help their children succeed in school and in life."

—John Sugiyama, Ed.D. Superintendent,
Dublin Unified School District, California

"Bravo! 7 *Keys to Comprehension* is the missing piece we've all needed for too long. This book empowers parents to take an active role in their child's learning, encourages teachers to validate children's ideas, and helps kids grow to trust themselves. It cultivates a partnership that will help *all* children succeed. Now we know how to work together to create a community of readers, learners, and above all else, thinkers!"

—Lesley Niboli Scheele, third grade teacher,
Newport, New Hampshire

"7 *Keys to Comprehension* is a ground-breaking, pioneering effort that reveals the 'real secrets' of literacy learning. It treats educators and parents as equal partners in creating a new generation of readers who are both ardent and competent. In clear, respectful language, it translates these secrets into something everyone can understand using interesting anecdotes, examples, quotes, metaphors, and suggested book lists and activities."

—Ann Fletcher, reading coordinator,
Maple Valley, Washington

"As an elementary school administrator, I envision a student body of engaged, excited readers who view reading as exciting as watching a favorite sports team. *7 Keys to Comprehension* is the link that will help educators and parents work together to build life-long readers who are actively involved with books and passionate about learning."

—Beth Peery, assistant principal,
Marietta, Georgia

"A marvelous book! As a result of using the 7 keys, our family no longer merely reads the words printed on the page. Books have become a part of us. They help drive our conversations, enhance our memories, expand our thoughts, and build our curiosities. *7 Keys to Comprehension* gives practical tips that will redefine mandatory home reading and forge a critical parent/school/child bond."

—Margaret Torres, parent,
Denver, Colorado

"*7 Keys to Comprehension* offers parents authentic, simple conversational activities to help their children understand and enjoy reading. From 'drenching your child with language' to asking questions, to determining importance, parents are given a rich menu for supporting their children's reading."

—Linda Pickenpaugh, literacy coordinator/trainer,
Newark, Ohio

"*7 Keys to Comprehension* is so easy to read and follow. I'll buy one for all my friends who have kids who are reading, so they can experience the amazing process of using the 7 keys with their kids. I feel more involved in my children's learning now, and watching them 'get it' is priceless!"

—Michele Strabala, parent,
Parker, Colorado

7 Keys to Comprehension

How to Help Your Kids
Read It and Get It!

Susan Zimmermann and
Chryse Hutchins

THREE RIVERS PRESS • NEW YORK

Published by Three Rivers Press, New York, New York.
Member of the Crown Publishing Group, a division of Random House, Inc.
www.randomhouse.com

THREE RIVERS PRESS and the Tugboat design are registered trademarks of Random House, Inc.

Permissions:
Pg. xiii: "I Love the Look of Words," by Maya Angelou, copyright © 1993 by Maya Angelou, from SOUL LOOKS BACK IN WONDER by Tom Feelings. Used by permission of Dial Books for Young Readers, an imprint of Penguin Putnam Books for Young Readers, a division of Penguin Putnam, Inc. All rights reserved.

Pp. 51, 78: "dandelion" and "sun" from ALL THE SMALL POEMS AND FOURTEEN MORE by Valerie Worth. Copyright © 1987, 1994 by Valerie Worth. Reprinted by permission of Farrar, Straus and Giroux, LLC.

Pg. 72: Illustration © 1985 Roberto Innocenti from ROSE BLANCHE, reprinted by permission of The Creative Company, Mankato, NM.

Pg. 85: Illustration © 1997 Janell Cannon from VERDI, reprinted with permission of Harcourt, Orlando, Florida.

Pg. 89:"Her Dreams" from UNDER THE SUNDAY TREE, by Eloise Greenfield. Copyright © 1988 by Eloise Greenfield. Reprinted by permission of HarperCollins Publishers, New York, New York.

Pg. 104: Illustration © 2000 Jim La Marche from THE RAFT, reprinted by permission of HarperCollins Publishers, New York, New York.

Pg. 152: Adapted from I READ IT, BUT I DON'T GET IT, by Cris Tovani, copyright © 2000, with permission of Stenhouse Publishers.

Printed in the United States of America

Illustrations by Nathaniel Levine

Library of Congress Cataloging-in-Publication Data
Zimmermann, Susan.
    7 keys to comprehension : how to help your kids read it and get it!/ Susan Zimmerman and Chryse Hutchins.—1st ed.
       p.   cm.
    Includes bibliographical references and index.
    ISBN 0-7615-1549-6
    1. Reading comprehension. 2. Reading—Parent participation. I. Title: Seven keys to comprehension. II. Hutchins, Chryse. III. Title.
LB1050. 45 .Z56   2003
372.47—dc21   2003006082

ISBN 0-7615-1549-6

20 19 18 17 16 15 14 13 12 11

First Edition

To Paul, who always read to our children
and charmed them with his stories.

To Steve, with love and heartfelt thanks
for believing I had something to say.

Contents

Acknowledgments

THERE IS AN old saying that if you find a turtle on top of a fence post, he probably didn't get there by himself. It took many years and the work of many committed, thoughtful teachers, staff developers, and children for us to be able to write 7 *Keys to Comprehension*. We are grateful to each and every teacher whose classroom we visited and worked in, the many students who shared their thinking and reading with us, and the folks at the Public Education and Business Coalition (PEBC) who have worked tirelessly to bring the thinking strategies to life in Colorado and the nation.

Special thanks go to Ellin Oliver Keene, who spearheaded the comprehension work at the PEBC. Her belief that *all* children are capable of brilliant thinking set the standard for the successful implementation of what the research said was essential to include in great literacy instruction.

We thank Cris Tovani for her encouraging words to write a book for parents so they could be included in the comprehension conversation. Cris's masterful ability to empower her high school students to think critically about what they read showed us how much could be done with students others had given up on.

Thanks also to Stephanie Harvey, who always raised the bar of our thinking, and to Anne Goudvis, whose thoughtful, intellectual approach made us probe deeper. Their conversations gave us insight into how the strategies help children access content-area reading.

We learned invaluable lessons from Debbie Miller, an extraordinary first-grade teacher who showed us how the 7 Keys unlock the thinking side of reading for her young students. Thanks for showing us all that is possible.

We thank all the PEBC lab teachers, who opened their classrooms to us again and again: To Leslie Blauman for showing us the incredible way her students respond to what they read. To Patrick Allen for demonstrating the power of comprehension instruction *while* children are reading. To Carrie Symons and Sue Kempton for their insight into the interconnected nature of reading and writing. To Barbara McCallister, Cheryl Zimmerman, Carole Quinby, Barb Smith, and Mario Giardiello for deepening our understanding of what works and how to do it.

Many thanks go out to the teachers in the Denver area and across the nation who invite Chryse to work with their students. Modeling comprehension lessons and hearing all the ways children think about what they read led to the creation of the classroom connection sections in this book. Holly Hargrove, Andrea Harris, Debbie Behnfield, Paula Bowers, Carol Calkin, Sharon Messinger, Peggy Jurgs, Margaret Wing, and a host of others willingly shared their students and their expertise, so that we could learn together about the power of comprehension instruction.

We are grateful for our colleagues at the PEBC. Executive Director Barb Volpe, Mariah Dixon, and Diane Sweeney make possible the structures supporting the ongoing investigation of this comprehension work. Lori Conrad, Director of Literacy Initiatives, always poses questions that extend our thinking; and Judy Hendricks keeps us informed and kept encouraging the writing of this book.

The encouragement and insight of PEBC staff developers Sam Bennett, Leanna Harris, Melissa Matthews, Ilana Spiegel, and Jennifer Shouse helped us realize the importance this information holds for parents. Kristin Venable reminded us of the power of listening as she modeled this talent with adults and children. Special thanks to Joy Hood, for her expertise not only as a principal who helped her elementary school implement comprehension instruction, but also for sharing how her grandson uses the 7 Keys to make sense of the world around him.

Thanks also to the remarkable teachers and staff developers who pioneered both reading and writing workshops in Colorado classrooms: The work and wisdom of Marjorie Larner, Liz Stedem, Laura Benson, Marjory Ulm, Fran Jenner, Bruce Morgan, and Colleen Buddy fostered the implementation of the these strategies so they could flourish in so many settings.

This work stands on the shoulders of great writing teachers who came to Denver in the early days of the PEBC, held workshops, and expanded our vision about how to write with and learn from children. We are forever grateful to Donald Graves, Shelley Harwayne, Georgia Heard, Ralph Fletcher, and Joanne Hindley for inspiring us and moving us deeper into the realm of thinking about what literacy really means.

It has been easy to be passionate about this work. We have seen classrooms transformed, children turned on to reading, and teachers reinvigorated about their profession. Excellent books have come out of the PEBC's Reading Project and, as a result, changes are being made throughout the country in classroom reading programs. Reading for meaning is taking its rightful place at the core in many, many schools.

Yet we have long believed that the missing link in the teaching of reading was the parents. Parents are in the ideal position to awaken in their children a deep and long-lasting love of reading. Many do; those who don't, can. Both of us are fortunate in that we've had perfect laboratories to test our thinking about what makes kids become passionate readers. Our own children, now grown or nearly out of high school, have been exemplary guinea pigs and have all become avid readers. Thank you Helen, Alice, Mark, Carl and Elizabeth for your patience, curiosity, and support. You all are the best! Loving thanks to

Katherine, Susan's handicapped daughter, who inspired Susan to start the Public Education and Business Coalition and pick up her pen in the first place; and to Chryse's sisters, Sara Messersmith and Laura Copple, who cheered each phase of the writing of this book.

Without the commitment of Stephanie Higgs and Betsy Rapoport, 7 *Keys* would never have made its way to the incredibly capable hands of our editor, Jamie Miller, and project editor, Tara Joffe. Thank you all for believing in the importance of this book and its message.

Last, but certainly not least, Susan's husband, Paul Phillips, has been the ultimate sounding board and editor, reading every chapter numerous times, red pen in hand, recommending changes to clarify, clarify, clarify. Thank you, Paul, for everything. And Chryse's husband, Steve, provided encouraging words each step of the way. "Write it down—you have so much to say." His nudges to "keep going" were invaluable.

Without all of you, we'd still be the turtle looking up longingly at that fence post. We are deeply grateful.

I Love the Look of Words

Popcorn leaps, popping from the floor
of a hot black skillet
and into my mouth.
Black words leap,
snapping from the white
page. Rushing into my eyes. Sliding
into my brain which gobbles them
the way my tongue and teeth
chomp the buttered popcorn.

When I have stopped reading,
ideas from the words stay stuck
in my mind, like the sweet
smell of butter perfuming my
fingers long after the popcorn
is finished.

I love the book and the look of words
the weight of ideas that popped into my mind
I love the tracks
of new thinking in my mind.

—MAYA ANGELOU

CHAPTER 1

Reading for Life

*Reading is the greatest single effort that the human mind
undertakes, and one must do it as a child.*

—JOHN STEINBECK

S
O, THIS MAN decides to plant a special type of bamboo. He
goes to his yard and measures an area 20 feet by 20 feet. Over
several days, he digs down two feet to break up the clay earth, sifts
the dirt, adds manure to fertilize the soil, carefully plants the bamboo, covers it, and marks off the boundaries. Every morning, before
breakfast, he carries water from the stream to his plot. He weeds and
waters and waits. Every day.

After a year, no shoots have appeared. A neighbor who has ob-
served the man's daily efforts stops as the man works away and asks,
"Why are you working so hard for nothing?"

"It takes time," the man replies.

The next year, the man does exactly the same thing. Every day, he
walks to the stream at dawn, carries the water, carefully soaks and
weeds his plot. At the end of that year, still nothing has broken the
surface. The same neighbor walks by. "Why are you wasting your
time?" he asks. "I have some good seeds I'd give you."

"It takes time," the man replies.

The third year, the man builds a small fence around the plot to keep out animals. Each morning he walks to the stream and carries water to his plot. He continues to tend it with care. At the end of the third year, when still no shoots have appeared, his neighbor asks, "Are you crazy? Why do you keep doing that?"

"It takes time," the man replies.

Three weeks later, the first small, green shoots push through the soil. They grow. And grow. And grow! Six weeks later, the man's bamboo towers over 60 feet high.

It takes time. This phrase has little credence in our fast-forward, sound-bite world, where a moment's silence on television is referred to as "dead air" and multitasking is a way of life. But during those years when it seemed the bamboo was doing nothing, critically important things were happening: The roots of the bamboo were spreading, branching, thickening, developing the strength and vigor to support the bamboo's future phenomenal growth and size. Only with watering and careful nurturing could the plant develop the root structure to support the towering stalks of bamboo. Every bit of the man's effort, every ounce of water, was needed.

For your child to become a great reader, her mind needs similar watering. You water your child with words—talking and reading. It doesn't take a lot of time, but you must never forget to water, a little bit every day, day after day, week after week, year after year.

STATE OF AFFAIRS

As a parent, you may be confused. You want your child to become a good reader but don't know what to do to help him. You're bombarded with headlines about the failure of America's children to learn to read well, and you fear your child, too, will struggle, or you *know* he is struggling. You realize how important it is to read well, but you're afraid to interfere because you're not quite sure what to do and you've been told that teaching reading is the school's job.

This book, *7 Keys to Comprehension*, removes the confusion. It teaches you how to "water" your child with words and books so that he becomes a reader for life. Based on cutting-edge research on proficient readers, which was synthesized by P. David Pearson and a number of his colleagues in the early 1990s, and after nearly 10 years of applying that research in hundreds of classrooms, *7 Keys* demystifies reading and gives practical advice about how you can help your child understand what he reads *and* love reading.

It describes what is involved in the reading process, shows that phonics and pronouncing words is only one piece of the reading mix, and focuses on the importance of teaching children not just to decode words but to understand deeply and care about what they read.

WHY IS READING SO IMPORTANT?

Even with the hard work and caring of many dedicated teachers and concerned parents, this country continues to have a reading problem. According to the National Center for Educational Statistics, 38 percent of fourth graders cannot read and understand a short paragraph of the type found in a simple children's book. Results from the 1998 National Assessment of Educational Progress showed that 60 percent of U.S. adolescents could comprehend specific factual information, but fewer than 5 percent could elaborate on the meanings of the materials read.

No wonder many parents are discouraged. But you needn't be. By doing simple things like reading to your child, sharing your thinking about what you read, and telling your child stories, you can help him develop the foundation needed to become an avid reader. By using the 7 Keys that great readers use, you can help him learn that reading is not a chore but a lifetime adventure.

> Even with the hard work and caring of many dedicated teachers and concerned parents, this country continues to have a reading problem.

Reading is fundamental to success in life. It's that simple. Reading opens the door to virtually all other learning. You have to be able to read to learn mathematics, science, history, engineering, mechanics, political science, not to mention to surf the Web or figure out how to operate that new DVD player. Basically, you have to be able to read to succeed.

Poor literacy leads to unemployment, poverty, and crime. According to *How to Help Every Child Become a Reader* (U.S. Department of Education), 43 percent of those with the lowest literacy skills live in poverty. Our prisons are populated with poor readers: 70 percent of inmates fall into the lowest levels of reading proficiency. Seventy-five percent of today's jobs require at least a ninth-grade reading level. American college graduates earn 76 percent more on average than those with just a high school diploma.

Reading is not an isolated subject but a critical means to an end. That end is a productive, enriched life in which your child can master complex information, pursue passions, and make a decent living. Reading opens the world of the mind to your child *and* greatly increases her life prospects. There is no doubt about it: The biggest gift you can give your child is a love of reading.

READING FOR MEANING

Teachers see the same thing over and over again: Amanda with blond braids hanging down her back, book propped on her lap, glancing up frequently to make sure she's appearing to do everything *just* right as she reads out loud to her classmates; Tremain with mahogany skin and big brown eyes, not missing a single word as he reads with little expression; Angelica with the long black hair clasped in a ponytail, reading each word aloud—all left unchanged after each reading session. These children *appear* to be readers. They are experts at the decoding game. There is just one problem: They don't understand what the words and sentences mean. They aren't *really* reading.

For years the common wisdom was that comprehension was "caught, not taught." "Throw" a child the questions in the back of a textbook, some hints about theme and character, and some skill sheets to complete. Somehow he was supposed to "catch" comprehension. Often, the result of this approach was not comprehension but boredom.

Many kids weren't learning to read well or developing a love of reading. They were just like Amanda, Tremain, and Angelica. They could decode but couldn't really comprehend. They missed out on the joy of reading, because to them the words were just symbols that held no meaning. They hadn't tapped into the fascinating thinking, the adventures, the interesting facts, the poignant stories held in the words. They knew the external side of reading. They could decode. But the internal side—the rich, engaging, thinking part of reading—remained out of reach.

THE 7 KEYS

Sounding out or decoding words is part of the reading puzzle but falls short of real reading. If children don't *understand* what they read, they're not really reading. If they don't unlock meaning as they read, the words are boring babble and they will never read well or enjoy reading. So, how is meaning unlocked?

In the 1980s, a breakthrough occurred: Researchers identified the specific thinking strategies used by proficient readers. They found that reading is an *interactive process* in which good readers engage in a constant internal dialogue with the text. The ongoing dialogue helps them understand and elaborate on what they read. By identifying what good readers do as they read, this research gave important new insights about how to teach children to read it and get it.

Good readers use the following 7 Keys to unlock meaning:

1. Create mental images: Good readers create a wide range of visual, auditory, and other sensory images as they read, and they become emotionally involved with what they read.

2. Use background knowledge: Good readers use their relevant prior knowledge before, during, and after reading to enhance their understanding of what they're reading.

3. Ask questions: Good readers generate questions before, during, and after reading to clarify meaning, make predictions, and focus their attention on what's important.

4. Make inferences: Good readers use their prior knowledge and information from what they read to make predictions, seek answers to questions, draw conclusions, and create interpretations that deepen their understanding of the text.

5. Determine the most important ideas or themes: Good readers identify key ideas or themes as they read, and they can distinguish between important and unimportant information.

6. Synthesize information: Good readers track their thinking as it evolves during reading, to get the overall meaning.

7. Use "fix-up" strategies: Good readers are aware of when they understand and when they don't. If they have trouble understanding specific words, phrases, or longer passages, they use a wide range of problem-solving strategies including skipping ahead, rereading, asking questions, using a dictionary, and reading the passage aloud.

Good readers use the same strategies whether they're reading *Reader's Digest* or a calculus textbook. One moment they're asking a question, the next making an inference, the next creating a mental image, the next synthesizing what they've read. Over the course of a few minutes' reading, they'll have applied all the strategies without having given it much thought. They use the 7 Keys unconsciously and fluidly as they harvest the meaning and significance of the written words on the page. There is nothing fancy about these strategies. They are common sense. But to read well, readers must use them.

Susan and Chryse have learned how to teach children to use the 7 Keys to become far better readers. At Denver's Public Education and Business Coalition, where Susan served as the founding executive director and where Chryse has been a staff developer—a trainer of teachers—for 14 years, the strategies came alive as they were applied in hundreds of classrooms. Using the 7 Keys, children of all ages have been turned on to reading, and classrooms have been revitalized. Students and teachers have experienced the impact of these strategies not only in reading class but also in social studies, science, writing, and math. The 7 Keys give kids access to information across the curriculum.

WHAT DOES COMPREHENSION LOOK LIKE?

Traditional definitions of reading comprehension focused on the reader's ability to pronounce all the words, retell what happened, and answer questions posed by a teacher or test. Phrases such as "Just think hard; just concentrate" were thought to be enough instruction for meaning magically to appear in the reader's mind.

Real comprehension has to do with thinking, learning, and expanding a reader's knowledge and horizons.

For many students, this advice was not enough. They played the game of "school reading." They could pronounce the words and respond to simple factual questions. But they had gained little real understanding or insight. After the test was taken or the paper turned in, the material was largely forgotten.

Real comprehension has to do with thinking, learning, and expanding a reader's knowledge and horizons. It has to do with building on past knowledge, mastering new information, connecting with the minds of those you've never met.

If from an early age your child understands that it's great to ask questions during reading, to make connections to her life, to predict what's going to happen, to visualize, and to have an ongoing dialogue with the author, then she will be well on her way to understanding that the point of reading is to gain meaning.

If your child begs you to "keep reading," chances are good she comprehends. If she laughs at the funny parts and cries at the sad parts, most likely she's making meaning. If she pulls out books to get information about zebras, cats, dogs, chipmunks, stars, it's a very good sign that she's on the road to understanding. If your child is engaged and entertained by books and pleads to be read to, most likely she "gets it."

DRENCH YOUR CHILD WITH LANGUAGE

The foundation for reading is created before your child enters the school door. There is a strong correlation between the size of a young child's vocabulary and later reading success. You need to drench your young child in language so that he understands the meaning of words and stories, so that he realizes all of the thinking that words and stories can generate.

You begin by cooing and cuddling and telling your baby all about this new world he has entered. You chant nursery rhymes and play counting games. You hold him on your lap and read to him. He sits between you and the book and sees the pictures and listens to your voice. He watches how you turn the pages and hears the rhythm of your voice. He not only listens to the words of the story but also hears the way you talk about the book, sharing your thinking. He feels the enchantment of language and experiences the comfort of being with the person he loves most in the world. You tell stories about the time your cat got caught in the attic or your dog got hit by a car or your sister stepped on a nail or your little brother picked up a wasp nest and got stung a million times. Things you think are white-bread dull, he loves.

He comes to understand that reading is an adventure. He has certain books that are his favorites. He begs you to read them to him again and again, until all you really want to do is hide that favorite book in Outer Mongolia, but you just keep reading.

You've shown him picture books. You've read him books from the time he was tiny. You've talked about the book cover, the pictures, the characters. You've shown him how to turn pages. You've chanted the alphabet and taught him the alphabet song. He understands the meaning of words and knows the power of a good story. He's heard you think out loud about what it all could mean. He goes off to school, and somewhere around the time he's in first to third grade, he starts reading all by himself. You've watered your child day after day, week after week, month after month, year after year. You've given him a solid foundation of language. It *has* taken time. But now his root system is deep and strong. He stands tall: reader, learner, adventurer in life.

Take a Little Time Each Day

In the best of all worlds, you would take time each day to read to your child. But there will always be days, weeks, months when work gets too hectic, illness interferes, a marriage dissolves, an unexpected tragedy hits. During those times, you worry about what you aren't able to do for your child, but first you have to survive life.

Don't despair. There is still time to turn your kid on to reading. It's important to realize that it doesn't have to take a lot of time. Just find a little time every day, even if it's only 15 minutes, to read with your daughter. Talk about what you're reading. Share what goes through your mind. Guard this time! That's what it takes to create the root system for a great reader.

During your daily time together, be sure to share the thinking side of reading, which you'll learn how to do in this book. By using the 7 Keys, you will help your child understand that reading is not a chore but a lifetime adventure full of pleasure and new learning. You can help change your lethargic reader into one who reads for pleasure. *Stand and Deliver*—the movie about math teacher Jaime Escalante, who taught ghetto kids calculus and helped them get top scores on the Advanced Placement exam—showed that it is never too late to learn. Late bloomers are just waiting to blossom.

GOOD RECTANGLES AND NOT-SO-GOOD RECTANGLES

Let's talk about rectangles. There are good ones and not-so-good ones. "Rectangles" greatly affect your child's language development and, ultimately, reading ability. Good rectangles are the dinner table and books; not-so-good ones are the television set and computer screen.

Yes, there are worthwhile television programs, and the Internet provides access to a wide range of information and to people throughout the globe. But children can waste huge blocks of time playing mindless computer games, and you know how much junk is on the

tube. Nielsen Media Research reports that the average American child watches about 25 hours of TV a week. And that doesn't include time spent playing video or computer games.

The problem is not so much what the children *are* doing but what they're *not* doing. They aren't romping at the playground, making mud pies, painting with finger paints, playing dress-up, building with Legos or blocks, helping you "rearrange" the kitchen cabinets, listening to you read, making up stories, playing Mother, May I? or Simon Says, reading, making music, getting exercise. They aren't laughing over the comics, following directions to build a model airplane, or passionately tracking a favorite story character into another adventure. Instead, they're sitting passively in front of a television or computer screen.

So, what are kids missing in terms of mental exercise and development? They're missing a great deal, in particular activities that have them organize information, gain understanding, use their imagination, and practice their own use of language. They're missing the joy of reading. They're not exercising their brains. It's like perpetually sitting on the sidelines and never getting to play the sport. Bench-warmers *never* get good at the game.

A large study in Britain called Language, Learning, and Education found that the most powerful predictor of a child's school achievement was the amount of time spent listening to stories. Another study, Meaningful Differences in Everyday Experiences of Young Children, showed that the number and quality of verbal interactions with adults helped determine how prepared children would be to succeed in school.

Dinner table chat, in which children and adults come together and talk about their days, ask questions, engage in discussions, laugh together, and enjoy one another's company, is a kind of family glue, as well as one of the best things you can do to enhance your child's listening, thinking, speaking, and reading abilities. The two "good rectangles"—the dinner table and books—can make a huge difference in your child's life.

If you're reading interesting stories to your child and if your dinner table is a place where questions are asked, ideas are pondered, good humor is shared, and a healthy dose of listening occurs, then the good rectangles in your home will go a long way toward developing your child's language skills and ultimately her reading ability.

MEANING IS IN THE MIND OF THE BEHOLDER

Readers usually grossly underestimate their own importance. If a reader cannot create a book along with the writer, the book will never come to life. Creative involvement: That's the difference between reading a book and watching TV.

In watching TV, we are passive sponges; we do nothing. In reading we must become creators, imagining the setting of the story, seeing the facial expressions, hearing the inflection of the voices. The author and the reader "know" each other: They meet on the bridge of words.

—Madeleine L'Engle,
*Walking on Water:
Reflections on Faith and Art*

It's important to remember that meaning does not magically reside in the printed words on the page. Meaning is *created* in the mind of the reader. Reading to and with your child and having *real* conversations about what you think about as you read expands his capacity to uncover meaning.

Reading. Talking. Listening. It sounds simple because it is, but you have to do it. You don't get good at much in life without practice. Arrange special times around the dinner table for conversations. Bedtime reading is always great. Children learn best in nurturing environments, so create a calm, cozy mood around reading. Turn off the TV, video games, and computer, or limit their use. Get your hands on a "great read" and listen to the voice in your head interact with the words and pictures on the page. Then share your internal dialogue with your child, no matter how young. Do these simple things and you will be on your way to creating a great reader.

HOW TO USE THIS BOOK

To help your kids learn to read well, you have an invaluable booster: the 7 Keys. These strategies are commonsense mental activities that good readers use to create an ongoing interaction with the words on the page to make meaning. Good readers ask questions, create mental images, use their background knowledge, make inferences, determine what's most important, synthesize information, and use fix-up strategies. They shift from one strategy to another, depending upon what they're reading and what they need to understand it. Basically, it's all about thinking.

This book will take you on journeys into your own mind as you read short, provocative adult pieces so you have personal knowledge of the 7 Keys and can then use them with your child. You will discover the internal dialogue great readers naturally use. You'll get advice on how to help your child use the keys to understand and enjoy what she reads. She will begin to develop her own inner dialogue as you share your thinking about a book's words and illustrations.

We target three reading levels—preschool readers, emerging readers, and advancing readers—and provide specific examples to use with children at each level. Throughout this book, you'll find examples of great books for you to read to—or with—your child.

You'll also benefit from concrete advice for parents whose children haven't learned to build meaning, parents who ask, Why doesn't my child choose to read in her spare time? Why does my child give up so quickly when the reading gets difficult? Why isn't my child more engaged in what she reads? Remember, it's never too late for emerging and advancing readers to learn how to think *while* they read.

This is a book about giving your child the roots she'll need to grow, develop, and flourish as a reader. It is about watering her enormous capacity to think, reason, and become a reader for life.

 ## Classroom Connections

Because of the critical link between home and classroom, each chapter has a "Classroom Connections" section for teachers. In it, Chryse shares crafting sessions—explicit instruction about reading—that she has used in classrooms throughout the country. She includes suggestions for teaching the 7 Keys, and important concepts used successfully by teachers across America. These practical ideas can help teachers launch the strategies in their classrooms *and* renew their enjoyment in teaching as they explore new reading worlds with their students.

Now you're ready to plunge into the 7 Keys.

CHAPTER 2

Motion Picture of the Mind

KEY 1: SENSORY IMAGES

All good books are alike in that they are truer than if they had really happened and after you are finished reading one, you will feel that all of that happened to you and afterwards it all belongs to you: the good and the bad, the ecstasy, the remorse and sorrow, the people and the places and how the weather was.

—ERNEST HEMINGWAY

THIS CHAPTER FOCUSES on the creation in your mind of sensory images—pictures, smells, tastes, sounds, feelings—a vital ingredient if reading is going to be vivid, exciting, memorable, and fun.

Enlighten Yourself First

I am alone in my small office with a book of Carl Sandburg's poetry. "Plowboy" catches my eye.

15

Plowboy

After the last red sunset glimmer,
Back on the line of a low hill rise,
Formed into moving shadows, I saw
A plowboy and two horses lined against the
gray,
Plowing in the dusk the last furrow.
The turf had a gleam of brown,
And smell of soil was in the air,
And, cool and moist, a haze of April.

I shall remember you long,
Plowboy and horses against the sky in shadow.
I shall remember you and the picture
You made for me,
Turning the turf in the dusk
And haze of an April gloaming.

—CARL SANDBURG

After one stanza, I am transported from the Rocky Mountains, which unfold beyond my window, to Midwest farm country. I picture the plowboy, a strong young man with dirt on his brow and a denim shirt wet with sweat clinging to his back. He is at his prime, slender, with well-defined muscles in his forearms. He has worked all day plowing. He knows he must finish this field today. It is spring. The sun sets. Tomorrow there is another field to till.

An older man walking in the countryside at dusk comes upon the scene. As the shadows take form, he sees the boy and horses across the field. There is no wind. A hint of pink still hangs in the sky, though there is a murky quality to the panorama. On a damp spring evening, the green of the field is streaked with brown upturned soil. Winter is done. It is a time of new beginnings. The boy has a oneness with the soil that makes the man long for a different era. In an industrial age, there is little left that is as pure and untainted as a young man planting his crops.

The image reminds me of Aaron Copland's music, quintessentially American. But I sense more here. In the second stanza, a very personal nostalgia surfaces: The man watches the boy and is overwhelmed by the passing of time. He would change places with the plowboy in a second. He would be young and vigorous, sweating in the April gloaming, planting new seeds. But his dusk is upon him. His cycle is coming to a close as the boy's and the earth's begin anew.

Sitting in my writing room nearly a hundred years later, I see the plowboy and his horses on a quiet spring evening when everyone else has headed home for dinner. Vividly, he stands silhouetted against the hillside that rises behind him. A dank manure smell is thick in the air, filling me with memories of my father, son of a North Dakota pharmacist, who spent his summers working on his uncles' farms.

"Those were the best times I ever had," Dad has said many times. Annually, all of us—my sister, brother, and all of the children—visit him and my mother in New Hampshire, where they live in a small town of white clapboard houses overlooking the Connecticut River. We pack all the cousins in the car and go to an ice cream shop connected to a dairy. En route, we discuss whether the pungent stench of cow manure is worth the excellence of the ice cream. As we pull into the parking lot, all but Dad hold their noses. He just breathes deeply and begins to reminisce, speaking of those long-ago summer days, his usual stern countenance overtaken with whimsy as for a second he becomes the young boy he once was.

The image of the plowboy transforms in my mind into the western equivalent of Sandburg's Midwest scene. Across rolling rangeland a lone cowboy rides, rounding up the cattle before winter sets in. I see such sights when I leave the Denver area and head west into the Rockies. Always I am inexpressibly moved by the image. Perhaps it is nostalgia, my wanting to reach back to a simpler time before clogged eight-lane highways and junk e-mail.

—SUSAN

HOW SENSORY IMAGES HELP YOU UNDERSTAND WHAT YOU READ

In the opening example, Susan creates a kaleidoscope of images during and after her reading of "Plowboy." One image leads to another as she moves from a vivid picture of the scene Sandburg describes to her father's boyhood summers to images of lone cowboys. Because of the pictures, smells, impressions, and mental meanderings "Plowboy" evoked, she has a deeper appreciation of the poem. From Sandburg's poem, she feels the personal passage of time and the price we have paid for our progress.

Susan has taken a mind journey that leaves her with far more than the image of the plowboy. The poem fueled a vast array of mental images and memories of her father and of the Colorado landscape, creating an unforgettable collage that will keep "Plowboy" vividly alive in her mind.

What Are Sensory Images?

As you muse over a poem, read a novel, or pause over a newspaper story, a picture forms in your mind. Certain smells, tastes, sights, and feelings emerge, depending on what you're reading and what life experiences you bring to it. Information comes to you through your senses. This technique, which is called visualizing or creating mental or sensory images, triggers a wide range of memories and feelings.

The same thing happens when you listen to the radio. Many people listen to "oldies" radio stations not necessarily because of the quality of the music but because those songs take them back to their youth. The songs become much more than the notes and lyrics as old friends, old experiences, and old loves are revived in their minds. The songs are memory machines.

> Sensory images *are* the cinema unfolding in your mind that make reading three-dimensional.

When Susan hears the first few bars of the Four Tops song "I Can't Help Myself," she's 16 years old again, dancing in the high school gymnasium in Woodsfield, Ohio, the boys watching from the sidelines as the girls dance Watusi-style to the refrain "Sugar pie, honey bunch." She can smell the hot dogs and popcorn that were sold at those dances and remember the Brylcreem smell of the boys. Better tunes come and go, but for her they'll never top the best of Motown. They're not just songs, but time machines back to her youth.

Susan's son and husband are serious Broncos fans. Whenever they happen to be driving back from the mountains on a fall Sunday afternoon, they have the radio tuned to 850 KOA and listen to every word, moaning, groaning, exulting. Though they are far from a television set or Mile High Stadium, they see every play. Paul is not only driving the car and listening to the radio; he's also watching a football game. Mark is right there with him, and has been since he was about 7 years old. The game they're watching just happens to be rolling in their heads.

If you can create that motion picture while listening to the radio, you can do it while reading a book. Sensory images *are* the cinema unfolding in your mind that make reading three-dimensional. They are critically important to children, because they make reading vivid and fun. As Madeline, a second grader, said, "When I start reading, it's like turning on the TV. I pretend to put a movie on in my head." Or Nicholas, who just started reading longer books: "In books, it's like the author is the writer and the reader is the illustrator."

When sensory images form in a child's mind as he reads, it is an ongoing creative act. Pictures, smells, tastes, and feelings burst forth, and his mind organizes them to help the story make sense. It is this ongoing creation of sensory images that keeps children hooked on fiction, poetry, and much nonfiction.

If children fail to create sensory images while reading, they suffer a type of sensory deprivation. They are missing one of the great pleasures of reading. It would be like walking into a theater, sitting in a seat, and having the lights go down and nothing come up on the screen. Children need to be taught that the words they read, and the words we read to them, have the power to create a movie in their minds.

A CLUE TO KNOW WHEN YOU'RE GETTING IT

Sensory images play a valuable monitoring role. Once a child understands that there should be a movie running in her mind, she realizes that something isn't right when that movie stops or gets fuzzy. She is aware that she isn't understanding and can stop, reread, look up certain words, or ask for help to get back on the comprehension track. Then the movie can start rolling again.

At night, all too frequently, Susan drifts off right in the middle of a video and realizes the next morning that she has no idea what happened in the film. She has to rewind the video to the spot where she fell asleep to get the gist of it. It's the same thing that happens when your mind wanders while you read or when you just stop understanding. The movie goes blank, and you have to go back and reread to retrieve the full, Technicolor glory.

Grace, a second grader, put it well: "It's like you're in the book, but you're invisible and you're watching everything but the characters don't notice you. Sensory images are like a movie in your head, but if you're just reading words, you won't get a movie in your head, so you have to reread. Sensory images make reading a lot of fun. If you're reading and then take your eye off the words, you will say, 'What's happening?' And then if you reread, you will get your movie back, but if you keep reading, you won't get your movie back."

WITHOUT SENSORY IMAGES, READING CAN BE A BLANK SLATE

At a holiday party, several of us sit on the sofa, dinner plates balanced on our knees. We begin to talk about how reading was for us as children. Marty, a nurse and a mother of four, blurts out, "I didn't enjoy reading until I was in college, Susan. In high school, I always read because I had to, or I just didn't read at all. I hated the assignments, especially the novels and poetry. I didn't realize till later that I hated them because I didn't visualize as I read. I saw nothing at all. The books were just a boring collection of words.

"In college, things changed. I'm not sure why. One day I was reading *The Great Gatsby* and I saw everything—Gatsby's place on Long Island, the car hitting Myrtle. All at once, I got it. I could easily have gone through college and never known I was supposed to visualize when I read. My 16-year-old son doesn't visualize. Guess what? He hates to read. I totally relate."

Kate, a superb third-grade teacher who began studying the 7 Keys in a group with other teachers from her school, told Susan about her first book group experience: "About 5 years ago, we put together a group in my school and met Wednesday afternoons. The first book we did was *The Bridges of Madison County*. I remember sitting in the small conference room and not saying one word the whole time. Afterward, a couple of people came up and asked if I was sick or something. Usually, I blab the whole time. But I wasn't sick; I just couldn't believe everything the others saw. I couldn't believe words meant so much to them. I'd never gotten an image in my head. I'd never known I was supposed to. For the first time in my life, I understood why I had always found reading dull and tedious. That meeting changed me forever."

> There are many smart, competent people who don't create sensory images when they read. As a result, reading is often a chore to be avoided.

There are many smart, competent people who don't create sensory images when they read. As a result, reading is often a chore to be avoided. Kate began using the 7 Keys in her own reading and now has become an avid reader who readily creates sensory images. Marty was lucky enough to have had a revelation in college that opened the world of reading to her. Hopefully, her son will, too, before he makes it out of high school.

It doesn't have to happen so late.

What Vivid Sensory Images Look Like

Let's take a look at the sensory images that formed when 11-year-old Alex read this excerpt:

Quickly Bilbo explained. They all fell silent: the hobbit standing by the gray stone, and the dwarves with wagging beards watching impatiently. The sun sank lower and lower, and their hopes fell. It sank into a belt of reddened cloud and disappeared. The dwarves groaned, but still Bilbo stood almost without moving. The little moon was dipping to the horizon. Evening was coming on. Then suddenly when their hope was lowest a red ray of the sun escaped like a finger through a rent in the cloud. A gleam of light came straight through the opening into the bay and fell on the smooth rock-face. The old thrush, who had been watching from a high perch with beady eyes and head cocked on one side, gave a sudden trill. There was a loud crack. A flake of rock split from the wall and fell. A hole appeared suddenly about three feet from the ground.

Quickly, trembling lest the chance should fade, the dwarves rushed to the rock and pushed, in vain.

"The key! The key!" cried Bilbo. "Where is Thorin?"

Thorin hurried up.

"The key!" shouted Bilbo. "The key that went with the map! Try it now while there is still time!"

Then Thorin stepped up and drew the key on its chain from round his neck. He put it to the hole. It fitted and it turned! Snap! The gleam went out, the sun sank, the moon was gone, and evening sprang into the sky.

Now they all pushed together, and slowly a part of the rock-wall gave way. Long straight cracks appeared and widened. A door five feet high and three broad was outlined, and slowly without a sound swung inwards. It seemed as if darkness flowed out like a vapour from the hole in the mountain-side, and deep darkness in which nothing could be seen lay before their eyes, a yawning mouth leading in and down.

—*THE HOBBIT*, J. R. R. TOLKIEN, PAGES 201–202

"What do you see?" Susan asked Alex.

"I see Bilbo and the dwarves clustered by the rock face," he said. "Bilbo is the only one who still has hope. It's a great scene of the sun setting. Where it says 'a gleam of light came straight through the opening into the bay,' I see them not far from the ocean. The dwarves' faces are getting more and more depressed. There is a jittery little bird, the thrush, twittering from high in a tree. I can hear the rock cracking and slight moans from the dwarves."

"How does it make you feel?"

"It's a gloomy place. I feel worried for them. I have this sense of slow urgency. They've been waiting and waiting. There's a sense of last hope. Then I hear the rock groan and shift and the door creaks slowly open. I hear the sudden excitement of the dwarves, and I see Bilbo spring into action. There's a flurry of activity as the door opens. Suddenly, the action starts and there is all this movement and it gets really exciting. I'm wondering whether they will go through the door to the darkness."

A vivid mental picture formed for Alex. He heard the twittering bird and the rock opening; he saw the red sky and the frenzy of the dwarves; he felt the anxiety of the moment. No wonder he's an avid reader who enjoys science fiction and fantasy, two genres that lend themselves to the creation of sensory images.

"What do you see when you read?" Susan asked.

"I decide right away what the characters look like. Sometimes I try accents to solidify my image of the characters. I try out their voices, high or low. I see their clothing and the colors they're wearing. I pay less attention to the background and concentrate on their faces. In the fantasy books I read, when the characters are going through forests, I hear them walking, the sounds of leaves, crickets, insects scurrying around. Sometimes there will be background music, a piece I know that seems to fit. I can feel their emotions from the looks on their faces. It's like the words create a world. I remember not liking pictures at the beginnings of chapters, because I'd rather create my own pictures. I wouldn't want to read if I didn't do that."

"Alex, when did you start creating such vivid pictures in your mind?"

"My parents read to me a lot when I was a little kid. They read real books, not just picture books, because I had an older brother and they wanted things we'd both listen to. I don't ever remember not seeing pictures in my head."

"What would you recommend for parents?"

"Treat your children like they will understand anything you read to them. Read them really great books and they'll understand. They just will."

Sensory images came readily to Alex and made reading an exciting, intense adventure. Unfortunately, they don't for all children.

IS YOUR CHILD CREATING SENSORY IMAGES?

If your child begs to be read to and bugs you to *keep reading* once you start, chances are good she is creating sensory images. If you stop and ask her to talk about the book and she gives you details and has a good grasp of the story, if she laughs or cries at appropriate places, then she's probably visualizing. If she is able to make predictions about the story, saying things like "I think so-and-so is going to . . . ," and if she reads out loud with expression, it's a good sign. If you ask her questions about the characters and she is able to describe them to you, she is probably picturing them in her head. If she can extend the story, go beyond what is actually on the page, she is probably creating a three-dimensional image in her mind that has more details than the book does.

Signs that your child might not be creating sensory images include a lack of interest in being read to or reading; inability to put into her own words a description of what she's read or what you have read to her; lack of interest about whether the story is finished or not; and an inability to describe the characters, setting, or what is happening in the story.

Talking to Your Child About Sensory Images

You can help your child enormously by sharing the sensory images that you have as you read. You need to be explicit and direct in telling your child what you see in your mind as you read. Here is an example of how you might talk to your child about sensory images.

My Life in Dog Years, by Gary Paulsen, is a series of gripping stories about relationships between various dogs and the author, who has traveled more than 20,000 miles on dog sleds in Alaska and Canada. The book opens with a chapter about Cookie, a heroic pup who saved Paulsen's life. It begins as the author heads out by sled to set beaver traps. At a river bank he stops, parks the sled, and begins to walk across the ice to place a snare:

> A rope tied the cargo to the sled. I threw the rope across the ice to get it out of the way. One end was still tied to the sled. I took a step on the ice near the rope and went through and down like a stone.
>
> You think there is time to react, that the ice will give way slowly and you'll be able to hang on to the edge, somehow able to struggle to safety. It's not that way at all. It's as if you were suddenly standing on air. The bottom drops out and you go down.
>
> I was wearing heavy clothing and a parka. It gathered water like a sponge and took me down faster.
>
> —"COOKIE," MY LIFE IN DOG YEARS, GARY PAULSEN, PAGE 5

Let's say you're reading this story to your child. At this section, you could pause and say something like this: "I can just see Paulsen casually throw the rope out and walk across the ice toward the beaver lodge. He's striding out because he has a lot to do. All of a sudden, I hear an awful crunch. I see him break through the ice. It happens so fast. Boom! He goes down. I have an awful feeling. I'm afraid he'll die. Then I think of how I feel on a really hot day at the pool, when I just jump in and it's so freezing it takes my breath away. But this is much, much worse, because the water is a lot colder and he can't swim over to the side to get out, because he's weighted down with his soaked clothes and the ice is too thick over by the shore. He has to get out from the hole he fell through, but if he tries to, more ice will break. It's so cold. He doesn't have much time."

In a few sentences, you've articulated many thoughts that went through your mind as you read. You've seen the disaster unfold, felt the cold, heard the crack of ice, felt fear and sorrow about the potential outcome. You've connected to your prior knowledge about how cold it can be to plunge into water (even in the heat of summer). You've painted a graphic picture of what you've read and you've shown your child your thought processes as a reader.

Ask what your child feels. Ask what he sees. If he bugs you to *keep reading*, that's good. He's hooked and he wants to know what's going to happen. Keep reading. Talk to him when you've finished the chapter. Ask him to tell you what he saw. Add other thoughts that came to you as you read. Tell about your grandfather's favorite old mutt or the time you almost drowned. Share what you see in your mind and feel in your heart. Your child will begin to understand that words unleash a flood of images.

There are many ways to plant seeds that will heighten your child's awareness of sensory images. When you read to him, try this: Tell your child that you're going to read a story, and you want him to close his eyes as you read. Read a few lines, stop, and describe in as great detail as possible all that you "see in your mind." Feel free to go beyond what is on the page. Elaborate. Be creative. Tell him every sound you heard, every smell you smelled, every scene you saw. Do this again and again, so that you model what is going on in your mind as you read. It won't interrupt the reading. It will enhance it.

> There are many ways to plant seeds that will heighten your child's awareness of sensory images.

Now switch roles. Read a couple of paragraphs and ask him to tell you everything he sees. Let him be ridiculous. Laugh. You are watering his imagination. He is coming to realize the magic of the written word. Play it as a game: "Here's what I see in my mind." You can play this game way before your child learns to read on his own. You are showing him that books are much more than a bunch of words. They are keys that unlock the imagination.

MAKING READING COME ALIVE

Susan's friend Wendell read all the Laura Ingalls Wilder *Little House on the Prairie* stories when she was eight and nine.

"I remember them vividly," Wendell said. "Every night I'd fall asleep pretending I was Laura. I'd get up and sketch pictures of the house, the barn, the clothes Laura wore. I felt ripped off that I was a kid in the 1960s instead of the 1880s."

As an adult, she remembered those books in remarkable detail. Why? Because she'd created a three-dimensional world, and she'd been a player in the stories.

Encouraging your child to draw pictures is a great way to nurture her creation of sensory images. Keep a notebook by her bed and have her draw pictures of what she "sees" when you read to her or when she reads herself. Let her know how much you value what she sees, smells, tastes, hears, and feels.

Act out what you read. This does not have to be elaborate. For the Gary Paulsen story "Cookie," extracted on page 26, you could say, "This is what it looks like to me." Then stand up, pretend you're throwing the rope out, walk out on the ice, fall through, flail your arms in panic, grab the rope, and so on. You don't have to be Meryl Streep to pull it off. In fact, if your child starts laughing hysterically, you've probably done a great job. Or turn the tables and ask your child to act it out. You'll be surprised at how original she can be.

Don't make your time with your child feel like a bad day at school. Don't let your child think that reading at home is just another assignment and Mom or Dad is the teacher. Reading should be sheer pleasure, not a chore, not homework. Your kids will have plenty of homework to contend with over the course of their lives.

As you read together, you can say things like "Wow! Did you get the same picture in your head that I got?" and then describe what you saw. You can stop and act it out. You can pull out the sketch pad and say, "I'm a lousy artist, but you're amazing. What did that scene look like to you? Can you draw it for me?" Mainly, talk to your children

What Kids Say

Sensory Images

- "You get more into the story, you listen better, and the story comes alive."

- "You make mental images all the time, not just when you're reading."

- "Sometimes your mental images change as you get further into a book."

- "It's not just like seeing a picture, but making the picture in your head. It starts getting bigger and bigger. The picture is changing after you read more and more."

- "You've got to listen to the words, and then you get a picture in your head."

- "Mental images are alive in your head, like a movie screen is."

- "The more books you read in a series, the better your image gets because you really get to know the characters well."

- "You have to use your imagination to make a mental image."

—FROM BARB SMITH'S SECOND-GRADE CLASS

about all the images that come to mind as you read, and listen to them as they share what comes to theirs.

TIPS FOR PARENTS: CREATING SENSORY IMAGES WITH PICTURE BOOKS

The large children's sections in bookstores and libraries reflect the popularity of picture books. Picture books captivate readers of all ages, and

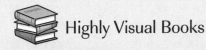 Highly Visual Books

Picture Books

Miss Rumphius, Barbara Cooney

When Grampa Kissed His Elbow, Cynthia DeFelice

Tar Beach, Faith Ringgold

Home Place, Crescent Dragonwagon

Tales of a Gambling Grandma, Dayal Kaur Khalsa

Longer Books

Grassroots, Carl Sandburg (poetry)

The Van Gogh Cafe, Cynthia Rylant (53 pages)

The Whipping Boy, Sid Fleischman (89 pages)

Because of Winn Dixie, Kate DiCamillo (182 pages)

Julie of the Wolves, Jean Craighead George (170 pages)

The Ancient One, T. A. Barron (367 pages)

many are well written and engaging. Sharing picture books with your child provides an excellent vehicle for showing your unique sensory responses to the words and illustrations. You can admire the pictures and words *and* still talk about the movie unwinding in your head. These books are stepping-stones to longer texts; as your child learns to visualize in shorter pieces, he can readily transfer this strategy to longer books.

Also, your child is more likely to remember new factual information in nonfiction books if he tries to "see" this information as it is presented. Knowing how to create mental images can be a useful self-monitoring device when challenging vocabulary or new concepts blur the mental picture.

For Preschool Readers

Read picture books to your preschooler. As you read, talk about what you see in your mind, then ask him what he sees. Look at the pictures together. Tell him what the pictures make you see, smell, taste, and feel.

Together, look at wordless books (pictures only, no text). Talk about what the pictures mean to you and what they make you think, feel, envision, hear. In Emily Arnold McCully's *Four Hungry Kittens*, the story unfolds as the "reader" discovers that a litter of hungry kittens wait for their mama, who has been accidentally shut up in the barn's feed room. The illustrations provide a perfect vehicle for you and your child to practice elaborating on mind pictures as both of you describe the scenes and action in your own words.

One page shows half the mother cat as the exiting farmer mistakenly kicks the barn door shut. You might say, "I hear that barn door bang shut as the farmer slams it with his big boot. I see the huge lock close tight with the mother cat trapped inside. Look at the heavy milk pail he carries. Can't you just hear milk sloshing inside?

"Oh, no! The farmer is all caught up in his chores. He probably won't even notice there's a cat trapped in his barn. I can see his dog running ahead, circling back, doing all he can to have his head rubbed or a stick thrown. That dog is full of energy. What do you see and hear on the next page?"

This type of conversation is an excellent way to encourage the creation of mental images in your preschool-age child.

For Emerging Readers

Readers of picture books create mental images that go beyond the illustration on the page. Talk to your child about those images. In Dayal Kaur Khalsa's *Tales of a Gambling Grandma*, we're shown the picture of a grandmother's bedside table, but not what's in the drawers:

First there was the smell of sweet perfume and musty old pennies. Then there was a tiny dark blue bottle of Evening in Paris cologne, shaped like a seashell; a square snapshot of my grandma holding me as a baby; big, thick, wriggly legged black hairpins: and stuck in corners so I had to use the hairpins to get them out, dull brown dusty pennies.

—*TALES OF A GAMBLING GRANDMA*, DAYAL KAUR KHALSA, PAGE 10

It might destroy this piece to pause and talk about each of its many sensory images, so you might want to select the words or phrases that give you a particularly vivid mental image and share with your child the picture these words paint. Here is Chryse's response:

When I read the words "big, thick, wriggly legged black hairpins," I thought of my grandmother. When we visited her house in Kentucky, all the cousins would watch her fix her hair in the morning. She'd stand in front of the mirror, reaching for those big hairpins to stick in the bun she built on top of her head. With each twist of her fingers, she'd push those pins in around the strands of hair. Thinking about that long-ago memory helps me see those hairpins in the drawer of this story.

Pausing to talk about your images will give your child permission to try this for herself. It's great if your child has different images. She should and will. Recalling shared experiences while at the same time marveling at each unique sensory image reinforces the idea that we are all different as readers. The important thing is to make sure your child turns on her movie camera. Understanding and enjoyment will follow!

For Advancing Readers

Once your child makes the jump to longer books, creating sensory images becomes even more critical in helping him remember and understand a more complicated story line. If he keeps a movie playing in his head, he will have a much better grasp of the overall story. He forms judgments about plot, character, motives, and action based on feelings and pictures he creates from the words. Reading aloud together (taking turns reading) and talking about the images each of you creates reinforce the importance of mental images.

In this passage from the first chapter of *The Van Gogh Cafe*, by Cynthia Rylant, we're at a roadside cafe:

> Once your child makes the jump to longer books, creating sensory images becomes even more critical in helping him remember and understand a more complicated story line.

. . . but anyone who has ever visited the Van Gogh Cafe knows that magic comes from a building that was once a theater; from a sign above a cash register that reads BLESS ALL DOGS; from a smiling porcelain hen on top of a pie carousel; from purple hydrangeas painted all over a ladies' bathroom; from a small brown phonograph that plays "You'd Be So Nice to Come Home To." Magic is in the Van Gogh Cafe in Flowers, Kansas, and sometimes the magic wakes itself up, and people and animals and things notice it.

—*THE VAN GOGH CAFE*, CYNTHIA RYLANT, PAGE 2

To catch the underlying importance that magic plays in this passage, your child needs to see the hints Rylant plants for the reader and then be on the lookout for the magical happenings that occur later. Visualizing helps your child start with concrete and move to more abstract thinking. You could say: "I can picture the inside of this cafe. I see a red sign with black print over the cash register. I don't have a pie cover for my pie plates, but I've seen ceramic covers with animal figures on top. I can almost taste that cherry pie underneath.

"Imagining purple hydrangeas covering a bathroom wall makes me laugh! Can't you just see those huge flower heads dancing across the room? I can't quite hear the music on the phonograph—it's not a familiar tune, but I like the title.

"I have an image of the cafe in my mind, but have trouble imagining what magic looks like when it wakes up. How can this happen? Perhaps magic will come from the ordinary things in this room, like signs, pie covers, and records on the phonograph."

A Big Step Toward Comprehension

These types of conversations go a long way toward helping your child understand the value of sensory images. But one note of caution: Thinking is messy. Comprehension doesn't follow a set pattern. The mind wanders over a range of possible pictures, connections, and questions as it seeks meaning. By hearing about your thinking process, your child will see that there is no single interpretation of what he reads. Remember, his response matters as much as yours. His opinions are valid, vital, and a key part of developing the confidence and thoughtfulness that will make him a better reader down the road.

 # CLASSROOM CONNECTIONS: SENSORY IMAGES

Is it possible to teach kids to comprehend? The answer is a resounding *yes*!

Showing students the thinking side of reading teaches comprehension. When you model how you think as you read, students learn how to talk and write about *their* thinking. When you pull your chair next to a student as she reads, you celebrate her discoveries and determine her needs. When you form flexible small groups to help your children internalize how to use the strategies, you are creating numerous ways for them to share what they've learned about the thinking strategies and providing opportunities for them to apply the strategies in all areas of the curriculum. When you give students long blocks of time to use the 7 Keys to build comprehension as they practice reading in a variety of texts, magic happens in the classroom. Students become more engaged. And with engagement comes deeper understanding.

Crafting Session

Students need to know that creating mental images is a vital part of reading and a key piece of understanding, remembering, and enjoying what they read. But just telling them to create sensory images is not enough for them to internalize what this means. Students need to watch you demonstrate *how* to create mental images. Thinking aloud will let them in on the sights, sounds, and fun of mental images. Crafting sessions are like bricks, each focusing on one concept that helps build the foundation of reading for meaning.

> *If books could have more, give more, be more, show more, they would still need readers, who bring to them sound and smell and light and all the rest that can't be in books. The book needs you.*
>
> —Gary Paulsen

Each mental images crafting session begins with a chance for students to hear about the detailed images you see as you read. Using all sorts of print—picture books, poems, newspaper articles, textbooks—talk about the images that appear in your mind and share your thinking about where, how, and why sensory images come to you. Invite students in on the fun as they begin to talk about, draw, and act out their sensory images.

Here's a sample readers' crafting session that explores the power of using mental images. In it, Chryse is working with a class of fourth graders and demonstrating how mental images enhance understanding.

I called the class up to the meeting area. "Come empty-handed, but bring your best thinking."

As I waited for the fourth-grade wiggles to subside, we talked about what we'd learned about sensory images. The biggest discovery so far had to do with where sensory images come from. The class wholeheartedly agreed that their prior knowledge launched many of the mind movies they create as they read.

Crafting Session Tips

- One image leads to another, helping you develop a deeper appreciation of what you read.

- Mental images are connected to your life experiences and memories.

- Mental images bring forth not only still snapshots of reading, but smells, tastes, feelings, and chills and thrills as well.

- Reading becomes three-dimensional when you call on your sensory images. It makes reading fun!

- Sensory images help you remember what you read as you personalize characters, scenes, plot lines, social studies facts, and so on.

- When your reading camera shuts off, it's a warning that there might be a breakdown in comprehension.

- Watching words unwind like a movie in your mind helps you stay with the book longer. You want to "see" the extended story or watch how science facts unfold.

- Using sensory images helps you move from a literal interpretation of the story to inferential thinking. You'll see the concrete representation in your mind's eye, and then extend the image to new thinking.

A week earlier, when I'd begun this comprehension strategy on mental images, I had shown only a few illustrations as I'd done the thinking aloud. I wanted the kids to create their own mental pictures to match the story. At this class, I wanted the children to pay special attention to the author's word choice, so I shared all the illustrations. My focus for the lesson was to model how strong nouns and verbs help readers visualize.

"Today we'll continue to think about how mental images help us as readers. I've noticed certain words help me visualize better than others. I think the author uses words to paint mind pictures for me. Let me show you how this works.

"I'll read from Marie Killilea's *Newf*. Notice your own mental images as you listen. I'll look up from the words, pause, and describe the picture I'm seeing in my head. I'm on the lookout for powerful words that help me see what's going on in this story. You'll have a chance to practice what I'm doing in your own books during reading time."

I began: "The wind from the ocean roamed through the house, and the remaining bed was a nesting place for raccoons." Some children closed their eyes to try to see the wind roam through the rickety house. The wiggles were gone.

On the second page I read, "It was a day in spring when flower and fern began poking their heads out of the brown earth. As the sea rushed to meet the shore, a large black dog was carried by the waves up on the sand. . . . He clambered up over the rocks and came to the deserted cottage."

I stopped.

"The word 'poking' is a great choice here. I know just what that's like when I watch in my garden for tulips and bleeding hearts to poke their way through the earth's crust each spring. The author might have used 'pushing up' instead of 'poking.' For me, 'poking' paints a stronger image.

"I can just see that huge black dog as it's washed on the shore. I can hear a giant wave crashing on the beach, leaving a dog behind. The word 'clambered' helps me imagine the dog moving his heavy body awkwardly in the direction of the abandoned cottage. I see him stumbling and slipping as he makes his way over the rocks."

I flagged more powerful words. Soon we had quite a list. The children shared mind pictures arising from words such as *bolted*, *crept*, *pounce*, and *buffeted*. Sara told us, "When I hear the word 'bolted,' I see the black dog jerk back in surprise. Just like I do when I hear a firecracker go off, or the wind slam the back door." The children spontaneously acted out some words. *Buffeted* sent us to the dictionary. We decided that an author's word choice has a big influence on the degree of detail we add to our mind pictures.

When the crafting lesson ended, it was time to get down to the real business of the readers' workshop: reading. "Today in your own reading, I'd like you to watch for words that paint pictures in your mind. Mark those spots with a sticky note, and keep on reading. I'll be walking around to hear what you've discovered. I can't wait to find out how this works for you. It's reading time."

A reading conference—a one-on-one conversation with a student—followed the crafting session. I pulled up my chair alongside Jason. He was reading Ralph Fletcher's *Fig Pudding* and had two fluorescent green sticky notes hanging out of his book.

"It looks like you've found some powerful words, Jason! Can you share how this is working for you?"

"Well, I marked these words." Jason pointed to *popped* and *gobbled*. "You see, the oldest brother, Cliff, has to cut up his baby brother's French toast, and even before he can finish cutting up one piece, this little kid gobbles it up. I think that's pretty funny. It really makes Cliff mad, because he's hungry and he has to spend all his time helping all the brothers and sisters. He's the oldest of a lot of kids."

"How do the pictures in your head help you make sense of this book?"

"I'm thinking that picturing that crazy breakfast scene helps me be in on what it was like for Cliff. He even had to look at his brother's runny nose as he tried to eat his breakfast. Ugh! I'm sure glad I didn't have to do that!"

I said, "So, picturing the scene puts you right in the action! I'd like you to teach the rest of the group about how visualizing makes you a part of the story. Could you do that during our share session? Great!"

The days following this lesson offered many opportunities for students to hear how visual images helped me as well as their classmates.

They practiced the strategy in poetry and book club books; they split into small groups to focus on specific issues and concerns; and all the students were given long stretches of time to read and create (and talk about, write, draw, or act out) their own sensory images.

Questions to Reveal Thinking

Here are additional questions to go along with this strategy. Each question would follow a focused crafting session in which teachers and students share the many ways they rely on mental images to build comprehension:

- What did you see when you read those words? Does having this picture in your head make reading more fun? How?

- Where is that picture in your head coming from? What words in the text helped you make that picture? How did your background knowledge add to the details of this mental image?

- Now that you've pictured what's going on in this chapter, what predictions do you have for what will happen next?

- Have your sensory images changed as you read this story? What words added detail to your mind picture? Yes, one image does lead to another. How do these sensory images help you understand what you read?

- You're reading a nonfiction book today. What did the author do to help you grasp the facts? What does it look like in your mind? Oh, you see a comparison of the size of these two plants! Please share with the class how even charts can paint pictures in our mind.

- I noticed you've highlighted this poem where the author used powerful nouns and active verbs. Did these words help the poem come to life in your mind?

- Great! You've marked a spot where you were confused—where you couldn't see what's going on. Why do you think your "camera" shut off? What will you do to get back on track?

- You've just marked and talked about two strong sensory images in this newspaper article. Does thinking about these visual parts help you come up with what is important to remember from this report? Can you explain to the group about how seeing the facts in your mind helps you decide what information is the most important to remember?

- Good for you! You've found a spot where you paid attention to the description of the scene in the story. Can you describe the image these words brought to mind? What did you learn today as a reader that will help you as a writer?

- When you pause to reflect about these words, what visual images do they give you? Oh, your response to this character is an emotional one. Good readers do that. They interact with the characters—almost putting themselves in the book. That helps us understand what we read. How could you describe these impressions about this character to others?

- We talked about how our sensory images deepen and change when we share our pictures with others. How has being a part of a discussion group helped you as a reader? Did your sensory images change after the share session?

- How is this working for you? Turn your paper over and tell me what you remember about your reading today. What do you notice about how your sensory images help you remember what you read?

- What advice would you give someone outside this class about how paying attention to visual images helps you as a reader? How would you explain *how* to create and use sensory images? What do these images *do* for your reading?

Teachers and Parents Together

- Host a family night, showcasing how much fun it is to activate and use mental images. Copy poetry and have families sketch their responses to the words. Make a collage of the various mental pictures brought forth by the same words.

- Ask local businesses to help purchase backpacks, picture books, sticky notes, sketch pads, and tape recorders and tapes that kids can check out of class, take home, and practice marking and sharing the images they see as they read and listen at home.

- Form adult–child book clubs to explore how this strategy works. Mark spots where you notice images that enhance your understanding of the story. Share these mental snapshots with the group.

CHAPTER 3

Making Connections

KEY 2: BACKGROUND KNOWLEDGE

For readers, there must be a million autobiographies, since we seem to find, in book after book, the traces of our lives.

—STAN PERSKY

THIS CHAPTER EXPLORES background knowledge—an amalgam of personal histories, all you've read or seen, your day-to-day experiences, your relationships, your passions. Background knowledge enriches everything you read.

> ### 💡 Enlighten Yourself First
>
> Chryse calls to talk about a class of third graders she worked with yesterday. In the course of our conversation, she mentions that she's rereading Wallace Stegner's *Crossing to Safety*, a book that I love.
>
> "Great book," I say.
>
> "Well, I liked it when I read it 10 years ago, but now it's totally different," Chryse responds.
>
> "Really. How?"

"Back then, I related to the college setting, loved the English classes and the relationships between the Morgans and the Langs. I could imagine the families vacationing together. But I skipped over the section describing the time in Italy. I felt sad about Charity's death, but detached."

"Tell me more."

"I was annoyed by the Italy chapter. I wanted the story to get back to the U.S. I remember talking to this neighbor who'd spent time in Florence and happened to be reading the book at the same time. She said how much she loved that part. I couldn't relate. The food, the descriptions of street corners, the smattering of Italian. There were no connections for me. Since then a couple of things have happened.

"Steve and I lost all four parents, so we have a real sense of what it's like to live with chronic illness. Now I know that horrible sense of helplessness and loss. It breaks my heart when I read about Sally's polio and Charity's cancer. The other thing is, we've been to Italy. I can picture Florence: the narrow streets, the Arno flowing by. There's something enduring about Florence that makes our time seem fleeting. This time, that was my favorite chapter."

"Almost like a different book, huh, Chryse?"

"Right! It's just not the same book I read a decade ago."

"You know what? I bet Wallace Stegner hasn't changed a word."

We laugh, struck by this example of the transformational power of background knowledge.

—SUSAN

WHAT READERS BRING TO THE TABLE

Background knowledge is all that you as a reader bring to a book: your personal history, all you've read or seen, your adventures, the experiences of your day-to-day life, your relationships, your passions. All of this becomes your background knowledge.

You might have heard the saying "Things do not change, we change." That might not be true with everything, but it certainly is with reading. Background knowledge colors how people read. Readers can reread the same novel, poem, short story, or essay and have a very different reaction to it each time because of new and different life experiences in the interim.

The meaning you get from a piece is intertwined with the meaning you bring to it. A layering occurs, a weaving of past with present, an amalgam of old and new ideas and experiences. As you read, sometimes you need to activate, or awaken, background knowledge, and sometimes you need to build upon it. You strengthen this process each time you read and each time you discuss what you've read. In addition, the very act of living your life adds to your background knowledge.

A first grader put it this way: "Background knowledge helps me make connections between what I read and what I know—little connections like 'I have a dog,' and big connections like 'pets that die.' Background knowledge helps me understand the story better."

John Steinbeck said:

A man who tells secrets or stories must think of who is hearing or reading them, for a story has as many versions as it has readers. Everyone takes what he wants or can from it and thus changes it to his measure. Some pick out parts and reject the rest, some strain the story through a mesh of prejudice, some paint it with their own delight. A story must have some points of contact with the reader to make him feel at home in it. Only then can he accept its wonders.

Those "points of contact" are the background knowledge that a reader brings to the story.

Chryse read *Crossing to Safety* differently 10 years ago than she did a week ago not because the book had changed but because she had personally experienced more of the events depicted in the book. New connections formed as she read. She was able to empathize and internalize in a way she couldn't have before she'd traveled in Italy or lost someone to a crippling disease.

SAME WORDS, DIFFERENT RESPONSES

Forty educators gathered in Denver to explore the thinking strategies. For four days they visited the classrooms of master teachers at work and listened to presentations, discussed, debated, and examined their own reading as they dived into one of the six books distributed on the first day. (Participants had been asked to choose a book and concentrate on one strategy as they read.)

The last morning, the participants broke into groups according to the strategies they'd chosen. Susan went from table to table, eavesdropping, then settled at a table where the conversation revolved around background knowledge. Several of the participants had read James McBride's *The Color of Water*, a story of his growing up as one of twelve children with a black father and white Jewish mother.

"I found myself getting angrier and angrier," blurted out Ruth, a dark-haired woman from Los Angeles. "The prejudice in the book made me livid. I could hardly read it. It's such an unfair portrayal of Jews. My grandfather was a rabbi and one of the most giving, wonderful people who ever lived. This book is one-sided and vicious."

"Boy, I hadn't thought of it that way," said Lila, a third-grade teacher from Massachusetts. "I was just blown away by his life, how he overcame obstacles. I just didn't see the racism you're talking about."

Ruth concluded, "I saw racism. It ticked me off. I ended up really disliking McBride."

Lila asked, "What about you, Barbara?"

Barbara, a tan, athletic-looking woman, responded slowly. "I have to take a deep breath. I don't know why I even chose this book. I started reading it, and my whole childhood flew up at me. Like when I read this, I just couldn't believe it." She pointed to a page and read:

The cafeteria at the Chase Manhattan Bank where she worked served dinner to the employees for free, so she would load up with bologna sandwiches, cheese, cakes, whatever she could pillage, and bring it home for the hordes to devour. If you were the first to grab the purse when she got home, you ate. If you missed it, well, sleep tight.

—*THE COLOR OF WATER*, JAMES MCBRIDE, PAGE 67

Barbara continued: "It's different, but that was my life. I grew up in east side San Jose. We were one of two white families in a black neighborhood. When I was little, we lived in a house next to my grandfather. He grew vegetables for the local grocery store, and when he delivered the vegetables, he always asked for their garbage— mainly produce. Our chore after school was to 'sort the garbage.' We found all the edible stuff. That was dinner. The rest went to the animals. We grew up with blacks, played, went to school together. We weren't into the color thing at all. I don't know how it was for my parents. We didn't have anything, but for kids it was a great way to grow up. Now I teach poor kids—some who live out of cars—and I tell every one of them, 'Hey, you can be anything you want to be. Anything!' This book meant a lot to me, a whole lot."

The contrast between Ruth's and Barbara's responses vividly demonstrates how different background knowledge shapes the response to what people read. Neither Ruth nor Barbara was "wrong." Both had valid reasons for their interpretations, and everyone learned from the discussion. Each person's understanding of *The Color of Water* was deepened.

YOUR CHILD'S BACKGROUND KNOWLEDGE

Talking about your own background knowledge with your child is one of the great pleasures you can share. You can tell stories, start conversations, read a page or a paragraph and say, "That reminds me of this book I read, or this story I heard on the news . . ." or "That makes me remember when . . . ." Sharing your background knowledge is a way to build stronger bonds with your children, to let them get to know you better and get to know them better. As your child listens, asks questions, and understands, she is not just gaining background knowledge from you; she is also sharpening and strengthening her own power over language.

When you read with your young child, look at the book cover together, read the title, the author description, the text on the back of the book. Discuss what the book might be about. Tell her what you think. By doing so, without even reading the first paragraph, you've built your child's background knowledge about what is to come.

Show your child how you read from left to right, how different types of books have different structures and formats. The format of a poem is different from that of a short story. Dialogue is usually set off by quotation marks. Talking to your child about these things further builds her background knowledge.

If you read a book about a dog or cat, talk about any pets you had as a child. If you're reading about going to the city, tell about the first time you saw a high-rise building or, if you're a city person, about the first time you went to the country and realized that there were open fields and forests. Share memories of your grandparents, your aunts and uncles, the family left behind in Europe or Africa or Asia. Talk about your friends and the silly things you did as kids.

> You might think you have nothing of interest to say to your child as you read. You're wrong.

You might think you have nothing of interest to say to your child as you read. You're wrong. Your memories and childhood experiences are fascinating to her. Immerse your child in your memories. It helps her build background knowledge. She'll realize all that books can spark while strengthening her grasp of language.

Building background knowledge is also a way for you to help your child pursue a passion. Kids have an intense natural curiosity. When some topic strikes their fancy, they instantly become motivated to learn. They want to know more, more, more. Your child might be fascinated with airplanes, dogs, outer space, rocks, electricity, the brain, Indians, mythology—you name it. You can help her develop her background knowledge about a subject by heading to the library and checking out all the books you can find on the subject; taking her to museums, parks, airports; reading to her; and just talking to her about her interests.

Activating Background Knowledge

Sometimes we need to help children activate their background knowledge. When Susan's son Mark was 13, he received several Harry Potter books for Christmas, devoured them in about a week, then promptly reread them all. What captivated him?

"Mark, I'm working on the chapter on background knowledge. You keep rereading the Harry Potter books. Is there something in your background that you think about as you read?"

"No. I just like them. I enjoy the story."

"Are you sure?"

"Yeah, I'm not a wizard. I just like 'em."

Several hours later, he reconsidered. "Mom, I've been thinking about what you asked. It's like Harry has two lives, one with this family that's not very nice to him and the other with the wizards where he's happy and has lots of fun. It reminds me of how I felt in school last year and how I feel this year. I really didn't like it last year. The teacher didn't like me. Some of the kids were kind of mean to me. This year it's all different. It's like I had two different lives. One was not so good, and now I have a new one that is good. That makes me feel kind of like Harry Potter."

Mark could relate to Harry Potter in a personal way. That made Harry's story more compelling and heightened Mark's understanding. Susan's questions spurred his thinking and activated his background knowledge.

WHY IS BACKGROUND KNOWLEDGE KEY?

> Although Cretaceous and Tertiary deposition has buried older rocks in the area under a sedimentary blanket many thousands of feet thick, an outline of the earlier geologic history may be inferred from deep well records and from studies in the surrounding areas. In the half-billion years from the close of the Precambrian to the end of the Cretaceous, this region experienced many cycles of uplift and submergence—but none of the great folding and faulting so conspicuous in the Appalachians, the Oachitas, and parts of Europe and Asia.
>
> —*DESOLATION RIVER GUIDE*, LOIS BELKNAP EVANS
> AND BUZZ BELKNAP, PAGE 51

There are people who understand the preceding paragraph. It makes sense to them. They can envision it and know how the geology of the Green River fits into the broader geologic picture of the Southwest. Even though this passage has already been "dumbed down" for laypersons, every time Susan reads it, she promptly forgets it. Susan has no background knowledge about geology, much less the geology of Utah. Without that background knowledge, it's like reading in a vacuum. Not only does she not really understand it, but the new information doesn't "stick."

It's the same whenever you read something that is totally unfamiliar to you. Let's say you pick up a medical textbook or a legal tract or a computer manual. If you have no background knowledge about medicine, law, or computers, you will have a hard time making sense of what you read.

Background knowledge is like Velcro. It helps new information *adhere*. The more background knowledge you develop and use, the more you can make sense of and remember new information.

MAKING CONNECTIONS

As a parent, you can encourage your child to make various *connections* around reading: text to self, text to text, and text to world. This will help your child become aware of the background knowledge that he already has and learn how to build his background knowledge.

Text to Self

With text-to-self connections, what you read reminds you of something from your own life. Chryse thought of her time in Italy when she reread *Crossing to Safety*. Ruth and Barbara connected *The Color of Water* to their own childhoods. Mark related better to Harry Potter because he, too, had been an outsider. Often text-to-self connections carry a strong emotional charge. These types of connections are particularly important because brain research shows that "emotions drive attention, create meaning, and have their own memory pathways" (Eric Jensen, *Teaching with the Brain in Mind*, page 72). Making an emotional connection helps us remember what we read.

Text to Text

With text-to-text connections, what you read reminds you of something else you have read or seen on television or at the movies.

A teacher read this poem to several 7-year-olds:

Dandelion
Out of
Green space,
A sun:
Bright for
A day, burning
Away to
A husk, a
Cratered moon:

Burst
In a week
To dust:

Seeding
The infinite
Lawn with
Its starry
Smithereens.

—*ALL THE SMALL POEMS*, VALERIE WORTH

One student, Zane, piped up: "'Smithereens' reminds me of broken glass or something shattering."

"What it reminds me of is those things you blow," said Janet. "Can you picture that? Poof! Then smithereens everywhere. It gives me a connection to Pooh Bear, too, because he tells Rabbit to eat everything but the dandelions, but he gets confused and eats them."

Felicia pitched in. "It gives me an image of something blowing away in the wind. There are all these seeds just flying around. Millions of pieces like millions of seeds. If you think of it as all green and then it turns all this yellow and then it's all these tiny flowers. It's just like the sun, because it's like the sun is right out in front of you. The sun is not up in the sky, but it's down on the ground."

Sean added, "You remember that poem we wrote about the man who came to class and told us funny stories? That's what it reminds me of."

"Yeah, I remember," Felicia said, and led them to where the poem was posted on a bulletin board:

Angel Vigil, funny as a clown,
turns stories into images.
We laughed so hard
Like a piece of glass
cracking into millions of pieces.

"Smithereens is like cracking into millions of pieces. That's why I thought of that." Sean said.

In a 3-minute conversation, the children created a vivid mental image of the yard sprinkled with yellow flowers and connected "Dandelion" to a poem they had written as a class, as well as to Winnie The Pooh. They made numerous text-to-text connections. And they made more connections by talking about "Dandelion" than they would have if they had just read it alone or listened to the teacher read it and then moved on to something else.

Text to World

When text-to-world connections are made, what you read reminds you of something in the broader world. Books, articles, and stories that make you think about something beyond your own life help you create text-to-world connections.

Danny, a middle schooler, read *Lord of the Flies* the month of the terrorist attacks on the World Trade Center and the Pentagon. Let's look at his response to the book: "There is the idea of a beast, something dark and evil and frightening, and it's like the boys are losing their identity and becoming the beast. It reminds me of how we see the terrorists as evil, but you break each person down and they have their own story and own life. Maybe they're not evil individually, but somehow collectively they become evil."

When his teacher asked what else he'd thought about while reading the book, he said, "Well, at first the conch shell is the symbol of power, but it becomes a symbol of weakness. To me, the conch symbolized civilization. It's really fragile and delicate. And in the end it gets shattered. It makes me wonder if what happened in New York and Washington and now the war in Afghanistan is like the breaking of the conch."

Lord of the Flies captures the imagination of adolescents and raises important social and cultural issues. Danny connected the story to the

> Books, articles, and stories that make you think about something beyond your own life help you create text-to-world connections.

broader world. That was a big part of the appeal to him. He could relate it to what was going on around him and what he knew about history. Talking about the book helped him crystallize his thinking and push his ideas further.

Show Your Child Your Connections

As you read with your child, you model the different types of connections by reading a page or paragraph and saying, "Oh, that reminds me of . . . ." Take the opportunity to talk about other books you've read on a similar topic, to discuss a newspaper article, to bring up things you just wonder about. This is your chance to tell stories, to share vivid memories, funny incidents, poignant losses. What you are doing is showing your child that reading goes far beyond the words on the page. It goes into your past and out into the world. It connects to books you read 20 years ago and editorials you read yesterday.

Talk About Making Connections

One morning, Barb McCallister read Judith Viorst's *The Tenth Good Thing About Barney* to her second graders. The story begins:

Background Knowledge Connections

Text to Self: You make connections between something you've read and something from your personal life.

Text to Text: You make connections between what you're reading and something you've read or seen or heard, such as a painting, movie, television program, or song.

Text to World: You make connections between what you've read and the broader world. These are often bigger "idea" connections.

My cat Barney died last Friday.
I was very sad.

I cried, and I didn't watch television.
I cried, and I didn't eat my chicken or even
the chocolate pudding.
I went to bed, and I cried.

My mother sat down on my bed, and she gave me a hug.
She said we could have a funeral for Barney in the morning.
She said I should think of ten good things about Barney so I
could tell them at the funeral.

—THE TENTH GOOD THING ABOUT BARNEY,
JUDITH VIORST, PAGES 3–5

Mandy raised her hand. "When I sit down on the sofa, my dog, Tango, comes over and sits on my lap. And one of the good things about Tango is when I'm bored, she'll come and play with me. I'm going to love her forever, and if she died, she'd always be in my heart forever and ever."

Then Antonio said: "I had a black cat, and my mom came home one day and he was dead. We buried him in the backyard. He died because a car ran over him. That night I cried, and I felt just like the boy."

Then Jordan took the discussion in a different direction. "My grandpa died. I think I was 5 or 6. It was really hard to see him in a coffin and buried in the ground, because I can't see him smile at me anymore. It just isn't the same without him. He shined like the sun every day. I know just how it feels when someone dies like the little boy's cat."

Jordan, Antonio, and Mandy had profound connections to *The Tenth Good Thing About Barney*. Talking about the book helped them remember poignant incidents from their own lives that increased their emotional connection to the book and deepened their understanding.

What Kids Say

Text to Self

- "I once had a word that I couldn't figure out. The book was called *Frog and Toad Together.* I couldn't figure out 'together.' Then I thought of my mom and dad, who do fun things together like Frog and Toad. I figured out the word!"

- "My background knowledge helped me when I was reading *My Sweet Sweet Tree House.* I know how it felt not to be let into the tree house because my sister and her friend didn't let me into their club-house."

—FROM PEGGY JURGS'S FIRST-GRADE CLASS

Text to Text

- "When I was reading *Ella Enchanted,* by Gail Carson Levine, I learned that the main character is given a gift at birth. The 'gift' of obedience turns out to be a curse she has to deal with the rest of her life. This idea of living with a spell granted by a fairy godmother reminded me of *Sleeping Beauty.* She was doomed to prick herself with a needle and then fall asleep. Remembering this story helped me understand Ella's situation."

- "I used to think it was really boring in colonial times. Then I read a bi-ography called *What's the Big Idea, Ben Franklin,* by Jean Fritz. When he was growing up, Ben loved to practice swimming. One of his early inventions was a set of paddles to propel him through the water.
  . . . Then, in *Ben and Me,* by Robert Lawson, I read the part about how Ben Franklin started to study electricity. My background knowledge re-minded me of how he loved to invent things. Facts from the first book helped me connect to new information in the second book."

—FROM LESLIE BLAUMAN'S FIFTH-GRADE CLASS

Good Books for Building Background Knowledge

Picture Books

Rosalie, Joan Hewett

Let the Celebrations Begin! Margaret Wild

Amazing Grace, Mary Hoffman

Lou Gehrig: The Luckiest Man, David A. Adler

The Lotus Seed, Sherry Garland

Longer Books

Exploring the Titanic, Robert D. Ballard (64 pages)

Neighborhood Odes, Gary Soto (poetry)

Bull Run, Paul Fleischman (104 pages)

The Slave Dancer, Paula Fox (152 pages)

Walk Two Moons, Sharon Creech (280 pages)

Through their conversations, they made the story more meaningful for the other kids in the class.

Children learn by relating their understanding of something new to what they know already. They need to process what they are reading, to talk about it, write about it, ponder it. This is how they make the connections that will allow them to remember what they read. When children are fed isolated facts, they might be able to remember them for a short time, but those facts will never make it into their long-term memories. A child is much more apt to remember stories, books, and incidents that are meaningful because they connect to other things in his life. Encouraging your child to use his background knowledge and continually add to it is key to his becoming an avid and thoughtful reader, not to mention an interesting and engaged adult.

The Talmud says, "Every blade of grass has its angel that bends over it and whispers, 'Grow, grow.'" When you help your child make connections, then listen with reverence and delight as he makes them on his own, you're silently whispering, "Grow, grow!"

TIPS FOR PARENTS: BUILDING BACKGROUND KNOWLEDGE

For Preschool Readers

It's easy to encourage your preschool child to make connections. At this age, she is the classic "me, too" reader, and she wants to do everything you—or her big brother or sister—do. She is building her background knowledge with every turn of the page and often wants old favorites read and reread. She is solidifying her understanding of how words stay the same each time you read the book. Just try skipping pages; she'll let you know she's been keeping track of the story!

Even very young children connect their lives to words, ideas, and pictures. Be encouraged when your child stops to talk about the time she, too, saw a boat bobbing on a lake or watched as a bee lit on a flower stem. These interruptions are actually an excellent sign. Making connections is what good readers do. Give your child the go-ahead by sharing your own memories.

Young readers enjoy echoing the train talk in Donald Crews's *Shortcut*. You can share the sound effects of the train's *wooo* and *klak-ity-klak* as you read the book together. You might open a conversation about the story like this:

"When I read the words 'We decided to take the shortcut home,' it reminded me of the time your legs were tired, and we cut through the church parking lot and got home the faster way. You were so glad to cut out those extra blocks of walking. We were saving time, just like the kids in this story.

"Thinking about *that* experience reminds me of when I was a girl playing with friends. I was late for dinner, so instead of taking the sidewalk home, I cut across a deserted lot. The weeds reached to my waist. It was hard to walk across the uneven ground. My heart pounded faster and faster. Mom had warned me about snakes and broken glass in deserted lots. I made it home without meeting a snake, but I never cut through that scary place again!

"Thinking about my shortcut makes me wonder if the kids standing on the railroad tracks will get into trouble. What do you think?"

By learning to personalize reading this way, your child will experience the rewards of being an interactive reader. Her connections will lead to predictions, questions, emotional responses, and deeper understanding.

For Emerging Readers

Just as your child needs to hear you read and reflect when a phrase brings to mind a personal experience or connection, he also needs to hear what happens when you lack adequate background knowledge to understand what's going on. Show your emerging reader how you build your storehouse of knowledge with each reading experience.

Jan Andrews's book *Very Last First Time* is an adventure about searching for mussels on the seabed. Eva, a young girl in northern Canada, drops through a hole in the ice to collect mussels. If you live in a land-locked state, it's hard to picture what's going on, because you don't have the background knowledge of what happens to the outgoing tide under the frozen ice. Here's what you might say:

"I'm confused when I read these words: 'She was Inuit, and ever since she could remember she had walked with her mother on the bottom of the sea. It was something the people of her village did in winter when they wanted mussels to eat.' How did they walk on the bottom of the sea? In the pictures, it doesn't look like they have deep-sea diving equipment. Do you get it? Let's read on to see if we can figure this out. We need to follow clues left by the author. Let's see if we can find them."

> They had come at the right time. The tide was out, pulling the sea water away, so there would be room for them to climb under the thick ice and wander about on the seabed.
>
> —*Very Last First Time*, Jan Andrews, page 7

"Well, I learned something new! Now I understand how she can roam on the seabed. Pretty amazing, but this makes me nervous."

You point and read: "The tide was roaring louder and the ice shrieked and creaked with its movement."

"Will Eva make it to safety before the tide comes in?" you ask.

As you share your thoughts with your child, make it a natural interchange. By doing so, your child will learn to build background knowledge and deepen understanding.

For Advancing Readers

When children face longer books, the prospect of wading through all those words can be overwhelming. Some children abandon books with the excuse that they're bored. The fact is, following a more elaborate plot structure is probably more than they can handle. Therefore, they can't seem to "get into" the book.

These kids need help. Background knowledge can be a key to get them hooked on longer books. Relating scenes or characters from books to their personal lives will help give them the staying power they need to become engaged readers.

Even when your child can read all the words in a book, it's important to continue sharing connections. Take turns reading alternate chapters, pages, or paragraphs. Have a stack of sticky notes on hand and mark the pages where you have connections. Share your memories. Encourage your child to do the same. Hang the sticky notes—"footprints" of your thinking—off the page like bookmarks.

A perfect book for readers to share experiences, connections, and memories is *From the Mixed-Up Files of Mrs. Basil E. Frankweiler* by E. L. Konigsburg. The idea of two children executing the perfect "run away from home" captures kids' imaginations. The hero and heroine, a brother and sister, choose New York's Metropolitan Museum of Art for their destination and find themselves right in the middle of a museum mystery. Their days are spent doing research on Michelangelo and taking guided tours with other schoolchildren visiting the museum. At night they bathe in the museum fountain, scooping up coins to use for food, bus fare, and Laundromat services.

You might mark this passage with a sticky note:

> Claudia hid her violin case in a sarcophagus that had no lid. It was well above eye level, and Jamie helped hoist her up so that she could reach it. It was a beautifully carved Roman marble sarcophagus.
>
> —*The Mixed-Up Files of Mrs. Basil E. Frankweiler*,
> E. L. Konigsburg, page 44

You might say to your child, "Do you remember when we visited the traveling exhibit of Egyptian artifacts several years ago? We saw a sarcophagus. Remember that carved mummy case? Thinking about that helps me picture the scene here. That's where Claudia hides her violin case. Remember looking inside the sarcophagus? Thinking about that gives me a sense of being right with Jamie as he stands beside the tomb."

By practicing this strategy with your advancing reader, you will help him understand how to use his own experiences, memories, and knowledge to deepen his comprehension.

CLASSROOM CONNECTIONS: BACKGROUND KNOWLEDGE

What happens when students seem to lack stories and experiences to connect to? Often, they *do* have stories and experiences but just don't

> *Remember only this one thing," said Badger. "The stories people tell have a way of taking care of them. If stories come to you, care for them. And learn to give them away where they are needed. Sometimes a person needs a story more than food to stay alive. That is why we put these stories in each other's memory. This is how people care for themselves.*
>
> —Crow and Weasel,
> Barry Lopez

know it. They might not know much about the Civil War, but they know about conflict. Start a discussion there. That can help them relate to the conflict that split the country. Then help them build the needed background knowledge by providing interesting materials to read. The goal is to feed students great stories and gripping information so they come in each day raring to learn.

Students who know how to apply background knowledge create a personal connection to the words. They begin to take responsibility for comprehending. They know when they understand and when they lack the background knowledge to make sense of what's going on. Such kids are not only better readers but— through their sharing of stories and personal interests—they are also builders of a web of understanding in the classroom.

Crafting Session

The following is a crafting session on background knowledge that Chryse did with a third-grade class.

After a week or so of studying background knowledge, the third graders had developed a working definition: "Background knowledge is all of our experiences, memories, and knowledge that we bring to our reading."

The students were comfortable using sticky notes in books to indicate their connections. Now I wanted to push them further and have them write about their connections. I did back-to-back crafting sessions on double-entry diaries. The students jotted down words or sentences from the book on one side of the page and wrote their responses to those words on the other side.

Crafting Session Tips

- Bring your background knowledge with you to everything you read. Your memories and experiences have a critical impact on how you understand and respond to what you read.

- Activate what you know so that new ideas and information will "stick" in your existing storehouse of information.

- Note connecting points as you read to help you better remember and enjoy your reading.

- Apply background knowledge to help you go beyond the words on the page, allowing you to think back to past memories and experiences, to remember and understand similar texts, and to relate to the world around you.

- When you lack sufficient information to understand what's happening, seek more background knowledge. Call on an outside source (teacher, friend, expert, dictionary, encyclopedia, reference book, and so on) to fill you in so you can carry on.

- Background knowledge is the cornerstone of the thinking strategies. When you know how to activate pertinent background knowledge, you see more detailed mental images, ask deeper questions, and are better able to extend your thinking.

I began with Allen Say's *A River Dream*, a story about catch-and-release fly-fishing. In his dream, a boy, Mark, climbs out of his bedroom window and finds his familiar city street replaced by a winding river, a fly fisherman's paradise:

Remember, you're not going to feel the strike. You're going to see it. When you see a fish take your fly, raise your rod. . . .

—*A RIVER DREAM*, ALLEN SAY, PAGE 18

I paused to share my personal stories about fly-fishing with my family in Montana.

"This reminds me of the time our friend Erik told me to watch the swirling waters between two boulders downstream from our boat. He knew the water between those two rocks was a perfect hideout for trout. I stared as he flicked his artificial fly exactly in the targeted spot. My eyes strained on what seemed ordinary ripples. Suddenly, there was a swoosh. Erik jerked on the line. He'd snagged another beauty! Thinking about that memory helps me understand the intricacies of fly-fishing in *A River Dream*. It's not that easy to catch a prize trout!

"As you read today, notice when your life experiences relate to the words on the page. Mark your connections with a sticky note so we can revisit them in tomorrow's workshop. I'll be conferring with you as you read. I want to know how your connections help you think about the meaning of your book. It's reading time!"

With those words, the students were sent off from the group meeting area to get busy with their own reading.

The next day I met the students as they gathered on the rug for the second of the two crafting sessions. We revisited the chart we were developing about background knowledge, where we had generated the following ideas:

- Each of us is different as a reader, because we bring our personal background knowledge to the reading experience.

- As stories are brought to mind from our reading, they can be turned into personal narratives during writing time.

- We create new background knowledge each time we read.

- We notice that sometimes characters from one book remind us of characters in another book. When we apply our background knowledge from one source to a different situation, it helps us better understand what's going on.

- Using our background knowledge helps us make good book choices.

I began: "Today we're going to write about one of our connections. Last night I thought about the two places I'd marked in *A River Dream*. I chose the one that helped me make the most sense of this story. Then I jotted down my thinking."

I showed the kids how I'd created a double-entry diary by folding my paper lengthwise and writing a quote from the book on the left side and my connection on the right. "Which side has more writing?"

Allyson's hand shot up. "The thinking side!"

I smiled. "Always!" I opened to page 26 of *A River Dream*. "When I read these words, 'So Mark rocked the fish, back and forth, back and forth—until the fins began to wave,' I thought of a fishing trip I took a long time ago. This is what I wrote:

> I know about catch-and-release fishing because my friend Darleen taught me how to fly-fish on the Big Horn River in Montana. We practiced our roll cast on dry land before even entering our boat. She showed me how to attach the fake fly to my fishing line. We spent hours watching the fly float downstream, keeping a sharp eye out for the strike, pulling quickly on the rod to set the fly when a fish bit the bait, and reeling in our catch.
>
> After netting the fish, we took its picture, and then returned it to the water. Pointing the fish upstream, we rocked its body in the current until it was revived and ready to swim away. Darleen would then say, "Catch you next year," and she meant it!

"It's easy for me to relate to this book about catch-and-release fishing. Like Mark's uncle in *A River Dream*, my family believes the real sport of fishing is the challenge of catching the fish. Then we let them go. But what if you've never been fishing? Were you still able to find connecting points in the story so that it made sense to you?"

A lively discussion followed as we noted how differently each listener related to the story, and how each of these connections is a personal way to make meaning. Michael remembered Smokey the Bear's words about preventing forest fires and connected that to Mark's uncle's advice on leaving the river the way they found it. By thinking about the conservation angle, Michael could better understand the idea of catch-and-release fishing.

The children returned to the various books they were reading and wrote responses that focused on the connections they'd made. During sharing time, Cynthia shared her double-entry diary with the class. On her quote side, she had copied the word "stared" from Jane Yolen's *Owl Moon*. On her thinking side, she wrote:

> One morning I heard the doorbell ring. I went downstairs. My mom had first answered the door. I stood next to her. Outside there was a lady with a camera. She seemed excited. She told us that she had been driving by and she had happened to see into our backyard. On our fence she saw a great horned owl! She asked us if she could take a picture of it. My mom answered: "If you want to take a picture of a plastic owl!"

This child's personal memory connected to the crux of Yolen's story. The whole point of going owling on a cold winter night was to "capture" an owl in a flashlight's glare:

> Pa turned on his big flashlight and caught the owl just as it was landing on a branch. For one minute, three minutes, maybe even a hundred minutes, we stared at one another.
>
> —*OWL MOON*, JANE YOLEN, PAGES 23–25

Now each time I read *Owl Moon*, I also remember Cynthia's plastic owl story. One enhances the other. Stories do take care of us, and recalling them helps us understand what we read.

Questions to Reveal Thinking

Have your students mastered the concept of using what they already know to better understand what they read? Here are some questions to assess their progress:

- Think out loud about what you did to activate what you already knew before you started reading the book. Could you share what you did to get ready to read?

- As you read that passage, did anything remind you of your own life? How does thinking about what you already know help you understand this part of your reading?

- You've just built your background knowledge about (whatever you've discussed). What do you know about this topic now that you didn't know before you read this book?

- What do you know about the way a poem is organized? How does that knowledge help you make sense of this particular genre?

- Look at all these connections you've made! Are there some that help you better understand these facts? When you think about your thinking, what do you notice about how background knowledge helps you decide what's important to remember?

- Good for you! You've just thought about how these two books are related. Why is it important to use your understanding about one book to get at the meaning of another book?

- How did thinking about what you already know help you figure out this word?

- How did remembering the last book you read in this series help you better understand this book?

- You've just underlined words that remind you of a personal memory. How does this connection help you think more deeply about the meaning of this piece? Does it make you come away with a bigger idea not directly stated by the author? What is your new thinking now? What have you learned about yourself as a reader?

- How does your background knowledge help you predict what will happen next? Could you share this new finding with the rest of the class?

- It was great to hear about your past experience with this information in the story. I noticed that after connecting this text with your life, you raised a question. Questions often come to us when we think about what we already know. Please share this with the group today!

- You've just described a memory related to these words. Could you see the scene in your mind? What do you notice about how our background knowledge creates mental images as we read?

- As you write your report, your duty is to provide the background knowledge for your reader. What information will you include? What does your reader need to know and understand?

- You've done a great job activating and applying your background knowledge to better understand this chapter. What advice about how this strategy helps you as a reader would you give to someone outside this class?

Teachers and Parents Together

- Send flyers home announcing, "BK is coming, BK is coming!" At back-to-school night, have kids share their personal insights about how background knowledge (BK) helps them better understand what they read.

- Invite students, teachers, and parents to share their areas of expertise. By forming clubs and presenting information, members of the school community can build background knowledge on topics ranging from photography to scuba diving.

- As homework, send home a short story for parents and kids to respond to together. With different-colored pens, family members can write in the margins their memories and experiences as they underline words that activate their background knowledge.

CHAPTER 4

Why, What, Where, Who, and How

KEY 3: QUESTIONING

The most important questions don't seem to have ready answers. But the questions themselves have a healing power when they are shared. An answer is an invitation to stop thinking about something, to stop wondering. Life has no such stopping places. Life is a process whose every event is connected to the moment that just went by. An unanswered question is a fine traveling companion. It sharpens your eye for the road.

—Rachel Naomi Remen, M.D.

THIS CHAPTER EXPLORES the importance of questioning. Asking questions is indispensable for creating and strengthening the reader's ongoing dialogue with the page. Questions help a reader clarify ideas and deepen understanding.

💡 Enlighten Yourself First

He came with his little girl. She wore her best frock. You noticed what good care she took of it. Others noticed too— idly noticed that, last year, it had been the best frock on another little girl.

In the morning sunshine it had been festive. Now most people had gone home. The balloon sellers were counting the day's takings. Even the sun had followed their example, and retired to rest behind a cloud. So the place looked rather bleak and deserted when he came with his little girl to taste the joy of Spring and warm himself in the freshly polished Easter sun.

But she was happy. They both were. They had learned a humility of which you still have no conception. A humility which never makes comparisons, never rejects what there is for the sake of something "else" or something "more."

—MARKINGS, DAG HAMMARSKJÖLD, PAGE 64

Markings contains reminiscences, observations, and musings that Dag Hammarskjöld, former United Nations Secretary General, jotted down from 1925 to 1961.

The entry above leaves me full of questions. Who is the little girl? How old is she? Who is the father? It *is* her father, isn't it? Where is her mother? Why did they go to the festivities late in the day, after most people had left? Who are the "others" who are noticing her frock? Why is she wearing a hand-me-down dress? Did the man and girl want to avoid being seen? What brought about their "humility of which you still have no conception"?

I'm particularly curious about the relationship one senses between the father and daughter. It is as if some adversity has brought them closer. Hammarskjöld paints an image, and we, the readers, are left to make of it what we may. Where are they? At a carnival? A park? Is it a special Easter celebration that they want to go to, but in an unobtrusive way, a way that allows them to enjoy it but doesn't call attention to them? Is this taking place in Sweden, Hammarskjöld's home, or somewhere else?

I want to know more. What is the little girl like? The father? I have a vivid picture in my mind of the scene—he is tall and slender; she has long blonde hair; they hold hands and create a world only for the two of them. How have their circumstances—their "learned humility"—brought them to a point where Hammarskjöld would observe, "But she was happy. They both were"?

—SUSAN

THE IMPORTANCE OF QUESTIONS

Questions lead readers deeper into a piece, setting up a dialogue with the author, sparking in readers' minds what it is they care about. If you ask questions as you read, you are awake. You are thinking. You are interacting with the words. In the entry above, Hammarskjöld's observation raised more questions than it answered.

For this short piece, Susan began the questioning process with simple, straightforward questions about who the characters were. She then moved to questions about the setting and the other people in the scene. Then she became more interested in the circumstances of the man and the child. She could only guess what happened to them. There is no answer in the entry. Nonetheless, her questions gave her a clearer picture of the scene and raised her emotional attachment to the characters. Diving in with questions—even those that are unanswerable—enriches the reading experience.

QUALITY QUESTIONS

Toward the end of Albert Einstein's life, he spent a great deal of time walking around his lab, hands clasped behind his back, mumbling.

His associates became quite worried about him. The day came when one of them mustered the courage to move closer. Straining to hear, he finally picked out what Einstein was muttering: "If only I could ask the right question." Einstein was fully aware that his greatest task was not providing answers but coming up with profound questions, seeking the *right* question, which would open up new realms of inquiry.

Young children are master questioners. In their quest to make sense of their world, they bombard those around them: Why are there clouds? How does grass grow? Why is the snow white? Why do geese honk? Do fish sleep? How much does a hummingbird weigh? Frequently, parents have no idea how to answer these endless questions. In desperation they might change the subject or come up with a feeble dodge to get off the hook. In fact, those questions show a child's brilliance. She just wants to figure things out. She just wants to know how all the pieces in her world fit together. Children have the natural curiosity of great scientists. As a parent, you want to encourage them to ask the *real* questions, those questions that really puzzle them, even if you can't answer them.

> As a parent, you want to encourage children to ask the *real* questions, those questions that really puzzle them, even if you can't answer them.

In *Sophie's World*, Jostein Gaarder's exploration of Western philosophy through letters between a mysterious philosopher and 15-year-old Sophie, Gaarder writes, "The only thing that we require to be good philosophers is the faculty of wonder."

Wonder keeps the imagination alive and curiosity well-tuned. Asking questions is part of remaining open to wonder and alert to the world around you. Asking questions is how you make sense of the world. Asking questions is about taking risks and pushing the envelope. Asking questions is about furthering passions and satisfying curiosities. Questions indicate engagement. They are a fundamental part of being human. They are a key ingredient in building superb readers.

Encouraging Your Child to Ask Questions

Start with a book, any old book. Look at the cover. Carefully. What questions come to mind? Look at this cover of *Rose Blanche*, by Roberto Innocenti. What questions do you have? You might ask, Why does the little girl look so serious, so worried? Why are soldiers sleeping behind her? Are they on a truck? It looks like some of them have bandages on their heads. How were they wounded? Where are they going? Is the little girl Rose Blanche? What does "Rose Blanche" mean? What is she seeing outside the window?

Using just the cover of the book, talk to your child about your questions. Make it clear that some of the questions will be answered when you read the book, but some might not be. Let him know that

it's okay to ask questions before, during, and after reading. Questions show that you're engaged and curious about the ideas, characters, relationships, and facts depicted in the book. Read the quotes on the back cover—in the case of *Rose Blanche*, "An excellent book to use not only to teach about the Holocaust, but also about living a life of ethics, compassion, and honesty." Your child might ask, "What's the Holocaust?" Tell him what you know. Start a conversation about the book, even before you've read a word.

You are teaching your child that asking questions not only develops a deeper understanding of what he reads but also helps him gather information and get himself ready to read. You're showing him that there is nothing passive about reading. It's an active sport that can be done lying on the sofa. Instead of exercising his legs, he's exercising his brain. But that great workout will come only if he's engaged and interacting with the page.

READING WITH QUESTIONS IN MIND

The philosopher Socrates never lectured. Instead, he posed questions; he engaged in discussions. He used to say that his art was like that of a midwife. A midwife does not give birth to the child; instead, she is there to assist in delivery. Socrates saw his task as helping people "give birth" to the correct insight, because real understanding must come from within.

Encouraging your child to ask *real* questions develops an environment of learning and inquiry in your home. Sharing your questions with your child, showing her that even *you* have questions when you read, frees her to ask her own questions. Some questions don't have ready answers, like why there is evil in the world. That's okay. What matters is to care enough to ask the hard questions. That's how people learn.

Kids can (and do) come up with their own questions as they read. That's one key way their reading improves. You can help show your child how to come up with her own questions. For example, *Rose Blanche* begins:

> My name is Rose Blanche. I live in a small town in Germany with narrow streets, old fountains and tall houses with pigeons on the roofs. One day the first truck arrived and many men left. They were dressed as soldiers.
>
> —*ROSE BLANCHE*, ROBERTO INNOCENTI, PAGE 1

You might ask, Why did trucks arrive? Why did the men leave? Why were they dressed as soldiers? These are not huge questions, but they are real. Chances are good that they will be answered as the book progresses.

Later in the book, bigger questions arise:

> Suddenly electric barbed wire stopped me. Behind it there were some children standing still. I didn't know any of them. The youngest said they were hungry. Since I had a piece of bread, I carefully handed it to them through the pointed wires.

Why are children held behind barbed wire? Who would do this to children? Why are they so hungry? These questions are more disturbing and lead to bigger questions about how people can treat one another with such cruelty, and even about the nature of evil. These questions don't have straightforward answers, but they do generate discussion and inspire thinking.

Discussion with the Author

Your child might not know exactly how to start asking questions. One way you can help her is to set up a dialogue with the author. If you and your child are reading *The Runaway Bunny*, by Margaret Wise Brown, you might say, "I have so many questions for the author. Why does that little bunny keep running away from his mother? What is he trying to find? Let's read the book first and then let's talk about all the questions we can ask the author."

At the end of the book, you could say, "Has the little bunny changed by the time he comes home and says, 'Shucks . . . I might just as well stay where I am and be your little bunny'? Is this a story about growing up? About wanting to come home in the end?" Ask your child if he would run away, like the runaway bunny. Tell him you'd be just like the mother bunny and follow him anywhere he went. Let him try to think of other places the little bunny might run to. Maybe he'd run to a desert, or to outer space. You can be playful with your child in talking about the book. Your questions are jumping-off points for going deeper into the meaning of the story.

ASKING QUESTIONS TO MAKE SENSE

What if you read a poem like "Sun" to your child:

Sun
The sun
Is a leaping fire
Too hot
To go near,
But it will still
Lie down
In warm yellow squares
On the floor
Like a flat
Quilt, where
The cat can curl
And purr.

—*ALL THE SMALL POEMS*, VALERIE WORTH, PAGE 9

In response to this poem, your child might say, "The sun is too hot to go near. It's a good thing it's up in the sky, or we'd burn up. But how can it be on the floor like a quilt?"

Your child knows what sounds logical and pauses to question what doesn't make sense. She's learning that her questions will help her uncover—and discover—what's happening in a book. Puzzling about how the sun can make warm yellow squares on the floor causes her to stop and think.

Her question might lead her to a revelation: "Light is coming through the window, like when we can't see the TV screen because the sun creates a glare. Wait a minute—the *sun* made the floor warm for the cat like a quilt. Now I get it!" Her questions set up an inner dialogue. Without this, she might have missed the whole point of the poem.

Play the "I Wonder" Game

Encouraging your child to ask questions as he reads is part of a larger task: inspiring wonder. There are so many things to wonder about: I wonder what a black hole is. I wonder why people risk their lives to climb Mount Everest. I wonder how life began. I wonder what happens when we die. I wonder . . . Before you start reading a book with your child, play the "I wonder" game.

Mordicai Gerstein's *The Seal Mother* is a folktale about a fisherman who on Midsummer's Eve falls madly in love with a seal who clambers onto a rock, sheds her skin to become a beautiful woman, and dances in the moonlight. So smitten is the fisherman that he steals the seal's skin and begs her to marry him, promising that after 7 years he will give her back the skin so that she can return to the sea if she chooses. Your child might say, "I wonder if a seal can be a woman" or "I wonder if she'll ever get to be a seal again" or "I wonder if the seal mother will leave her human son."

Later in the book it says: "There is a kind of seal called a selkie. On Midsummer's Eve, the longest night of the year, the selkies take human form to dance and sing. They love music." It also says the seal mother does return to the sea but visits her human son every Midsummer's Eve. Your child's early questions are answered as the story unfolds.

Questions send readers on *quests.* They cause readers to seek, pursue, and search for answers or deeper understanding. Questions also keep readers turning pages to answer the ultimate question: What happens? The "what happens" question is basic to reading fiction. You want to find out if the selkie will return to the sea. You want to find out what happens to Rose Blanche, or Frodo Baggins, or Harry Potter, or David Copperfield, or Don Quixote.

> Questions send readers on *quests.* They cause readers to seek, pursue, and search for answers or deeper understanding.

This natural impulse to ask questions and find out what happens is critical to making reading fun. If it's fun, your child will do it. If it isn't, he'll avoid it like the plague. If your child thinks reading is filling out worksheets and practicing vocabulary words, he'll never like it. No one curls up with a vocabulary list. Reading should never be a boring chore. You are the person to dispel that notion. Help your child fall in love with the *story.* Share the excitement, the questions, the playfulness, the pleasure of reading. Keep the sense of wonder alive.

The Power of Honoring Questions

An article in the *Denver Post* told about a longtime history teacher, Dick Jordan. Starting in 1962, he invited each year's history students to meet him on the steps of the Denver Public Library at noon on January 1, 2000. He jokingly told them each to bring along a dollar for his retirement. Nearly 300 former students remembered that request and joined Dick Jordan all those years later.

Why had they traveled from throughout the United States to rendezvous with this particular teacher? "He taught us how to question what was in the history books," one said as others nodded in agreement. "He wanted us to think outside the box before it was popular to do so."

Jordan's students never forgot the power of questioning. You can be the same sort of mentor for your child. Share your questions. Ponder them. Laugh about them. Let one question lead to another. Keep going deeper with them. Encourage your child to ask the tough questions. Remind her that questions lead to new ideas and perspectives. Let her know that even though there are not always answers, what is important is the quest.

 What Kids Say

Questioning

- "When I find a question in something I am reading, it lingers in my mind until I can't stand not having the answer. Asking questions makes me want to read further until I find the answer. For instance, I was reading *Dragon Steel*, by Laurence Yep, and I came to the part where Shimmer, the dragon princess, changes Thor and Indigo into fish. I was wondering why, if her clan eats fish, did she change them into fish. On the next page I found the answer. She changed them into fish so that they could swim faster to get away from their enemies. When I found the answer, my brain went, 'Aha! I should have known that!'"

- "Questioning in my mind is a type of thinking. When I'm reading a fiction book, I start to think, and when I think about a specific character, I come up with a bazillion questions, and if I think hard enough, I can answer most of them, but I still have two or three questions left in my head that keep me reading the book."

- "When I'm reading a nonfiction book, I have lots of 'what if' questions, such as 'What if there were no Indians when the colonists arrived?' The only way I can answer those questions is to put myself in that situation and think what I would do."

(continues)

- "My class and I were all reading history chapters. I was not excited. History was not a subject I favored. We learned about how to ask questions about facts in the chapter. I had many questions. I started to get interested. I actually started to enjoy history. When we were done reading three chapters, I had many questions. It made me want to read further. I needed to have the answers. Questioning has helped me to understand and read further. Now I'm a lot more interested in history."

- "I used to think that reading was boring and that there was no point to it. But now that I'm doing the questioning, I *want* to read. I like how I can ask my own questions. I used to get messed up on my words, but now I can ask questions, so it helps me read."

—From Carol Calkin's fifth-grade class

TIPS FOR PARENTS: ENCOURAGING QUESTIONING

There's no doubt about it: Kids love to generate their own questions! Questioning makes reading fun. But to know how to question, your child needs to hear your questions first. This is not about asking your child questions. Instead, it's about modeling what it means to be curious by sharing the questions *you* have while you read. Don't rush to the answers right away; let the questions hang in the air. Pose several questions and then let your child take a turn asking questions that come to her mind. You're showing your child how to be an active player in the world of reading.

For Preschool Readers

Look at the cover of Barbara Abercrombie's *Charlie Anderson*. You might say, "I wonder if the cat's name is Charlie Anderson. Or is the

Books That Raise Questions

Picture Books

The Sick Day, Patricia MacLachlan

Elmer, David McKee

Charlie Anderson, Barbara Abercrombie

The Bracelet, Yoshiko Uchida

Uncle Jed's Barbershop, Margaree King Mitchell

The Wolf, Margaret Barbalet

Longer Books

The Place My Words Are Looking For, Paul B. Janeczko (poetry)

Avalanche, Stephen Kramer (48 pages)

War Boys, Michael Foreman (92 pages)

The Upstairs Room, Johanna Reiss (196 pages)

owner of the cat named Charlie Anderson? Why is the cat caught between the bars? Is he in someone's bed? Is the cat poking through a staircase? Is it a boy or girl cat?"

Questions about the cover ignite curiosity about what will happen inside the book. Once you get into the story, the pictures and simple text unfold the plot: A mischievous gray cat adopts the home of Sarah and Elizabeth. After sampling their dinner and trying out their beds, he decides to stay. The girls call the cat Charlie. "Why does Charlie leave each day after breakfast? Does he like being dressed in doll clothes? Why is he getting fatter and fatter? I wonder what he does in the woods all day."

On a stormy night, Charlie fails to come home: "Where is Charlie? Is he safe? What do cats do when it rains? Will the girls find Charlie?"

Language to Use with Questioning

"I wonder . . ."

"Why?"

"What does this mean?"

"That was a great question. Do you have any more?"

"Your question made me think of another question."

"How come . . .?"

> *Much of what we know about intelligence and achievement shows that the power of what individuals know depends, in very large part, not on the information they control but on the scope and originality of the questions they ask.*
>
> —*Reading Reconsidered: Literature and Literacy in High School,* Dennie Palmer Wolf (ed.)

The girls' search for Charlie leads them to a new house on the other side of the woods. They learn that this family has owned a gray cat for 7 years, but his name is Anderson: "Is this their cat? Does Charlie live at both homes? What will the girls do now? What will they do if they have to give him up?"

Of course, your questions will be different. They will be your own, and they will help you uncover the meaning of the story.

For Emerging Readers

The risk-free environment of your home is the perfect setting for helping your child develop the powerful thinking strategy of asking questions.

In the book *Verdi*, by Janell Cannon, you and your child might wonder about a young python's struggle to fit into a world where he's encouraged to grow up big and green. The questions you raise might

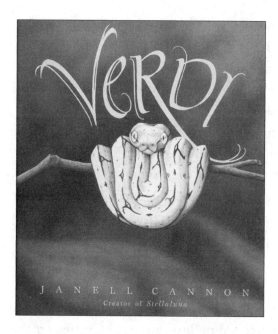

even lead to a discussion about growing up in the confusing world of humans.

After learning that Verdi liked his youthful yellow stripes, your child might ask: "Why doesn't Verdi want to turn green? Will he ever meet a grown-up snake he likes? What does 'molt' mean?"

Praise your child for identifying an unknown word. You can share what you know about the word's definition or decide to read on to see if the meaning is explained as the story continues.

As it turns out, the word "molt" plays an important role in the life of this adolescent python. The sentence "But one day, Verdi's skin began to peel, revealing a pale green stripe stretching along his whole body" helps answer the question.

The young snake tries to cover his greenness with leaves and mud: "But the soft brown muck dried into a hard gray shell and Verdi could barely move. If he even budged, the stuff cracked off in jagged chunks. As each piece fell away, Verdi could see that his body was even greener than before."

Your discussion with your child continues: "Will he ever be happy with who he is? Will he finally notice that being green is a good deal for him?" Your child might hit the nail on the head: "Does Verdi understand how important it is to be green instead of yellow? Now he blends in. It keeps him safe."

By the end of the story, Verdi accepts the inevitable by saying, "I may be big and very green, but I'm still me!"

Verdi's insight might (or might not) lead you and your child to discuss "growing up" issues. The important thing is for your child to learn to value her questions and be aware of how they increase her understanding.

For Advancing Readers

Your child is now facing the challenge of answering questions posed by outside sources. With little effort, he can answer the end-of-chapter science questions or fill in the blanks about an assigned novel. But perhaps he's become an apathetic reader and doesn't generate his own questions.

Let's say he faces a take-home chapter about Jamestown from Joy Hakin's textbook *The History of US*. If he can write on his copy, show him how to jot questions in the margins. If that is not an option, have him use sticky notes. You could read the first few paragraphs and say out loud what questions come to you as you read about Jamestown. Don't worry about posing sophisticated questions. Simple questions are fine. Let your child see how questioning helps push you through the chapter, allowing you to build a personal connection to life in the 1600s.

> Show your child how to notice when answers are revealed but also to be comfortable with questions that don't have easy answers.

You might say, "Why was Jamestown a wreck when the two English ships arrived in 1610? What is yellow fever? What was it like to be in constant fear of the Indians? I wonder how Lord de la Warr was able to persuade them to rebuild Jamestown. Why didn't the colonists go somewhere else to start over? Could *we* have stood all of this hardship? What did they do after they burned most of their buildings to stay warm? Will Pocahontas help the colonists?"

Now let your child take a turn at questioning. At this point, some of your questions will have been answered; some will be unresolved. Show him how to notice when answers are revealed but also to be comfortable with questions that don't have easy answers. Encourage him to react to new facts by forming more questions.

He might continue making sense out of this piece by asking, "Why did Rolfe need to ask permission to marry Pocahontas? How long will peace last between the colonists and the Indians? What was it like for an Indian girl to travel to England? What happened to her baby after Pocahontas died of smallpox?"

By paying attention to his questions, your child will become a critical reader of nonfiction. His questions create a personal link to this slice of history. Looking back over his questions, he can reflect on his thinking and then form conclusions or generate deeper questions. He'll find answers as he creates questions that matter to him.

 ## CLASSROOM CONNECTIONS: QUESTIONING

> *Education is not the filling of a pail but the lighting of a fire.*
>
> —William Butler Yeats

For students to become passionate learners, teachers must ask themselves one simple question: Who owns the questions in our classroom? The answer is equally simple: The learners must.

Questions abound in classrooms. They are at the end of social studies chapters, accompany science experiments, are handed out during a novel study, and are part of many prepackaged work-your-way-to-the-next-color reading series. But the definition of this strategy is straightforward and has nothing to do with questions posed by an outside source. Good readers generate questions before, during, and after reading.

Your job as teacher is to show students the way and then get out of the way. You model how questions come to you and demonstrate

Crafting Session Tips

- Your questions help you interact with the author, discover what you care about, and help you figure out what you want to learn. Questions help you make sense of your reading.

- Questions keep your mind alert as you interact with the words.

- When you dive in with questions, your reading is enriched.

- Your best questions are ones you truly care about.

- Some questions don't have easy answers. But all questions inspire thinking, generate discussion, or lead you to other sources.

- Questions are jumping-off points for going deeper into the meaning of the story or the information being learned.

- Questions keep you turning the pages to find out what happens next. Questions send you on a search for answers.

- Questions lead you to new ideas, new perspectives, and additional questions.

ways to record those questions. You stock the classroom with materials worthy of children's curiosity, give them extended time to question what's curious to them, and provide ways to "go public" with their learning. When kids know their questions matter, their fire is lit.

Crafting Session

Here is a crafting session teachers might model to show kids how questions help us understand poetry.

Chryse was a guest teacher in this second-grade class and was in the third week of working on questioning. The children had practiced using sticky notes to flag their questions in books they were reading. Together we had listed our questions on chart paper and then discussed whether they were answered in the book or in our heads, or whether we had to go to an outside source. We had discussed whether our personal questions were "thin" (easy to clarify by reading further or looking up a word) or "thick" (deeper questions dealing more with ideas and imponderables). Our questions tended to be "thicker" as the story progressed or as we got further into our topic. So far, we had posted three guidelines about questioning:

1. There's no such thing as a dumb question.
2. Ask questions that really matter to you.
3. Ask questions when reading doesn't make sense.

Poetry often packs a fertile field of questions in a small amount of space. Because the second graders were ready for a new challenge, I copied a poem on large chart paper, leaving plenty of white space around the edges to jot my questions. With children sitting close to the easel and the poem at their eye level, I read it twice out loud.

Her Dreams
In her dreams
there are sometimes trees
on which hang ornaments
as tall as she
she lifts her arms
to touch them
if she can stretch
high enough to
claim them
they will become
the jeweled moments
of her life.

—*UNDER THE SUNDAY TREE*, ELOISE GREENFIELD, PAGE 10

After the second read-through, I told them I was going to remember my thinking by "leaving tracks in the snow"—writing my questions in the margins. I wrote: "I wonder what these ornaments are doing on the trees. Why are the ornaments so tall? What does it mean to claim them? How high must she stretch to claim the ornaments? What is a jeweled moment? Are jeweled moments good things? Is this a sleeping-type dream, or life-goal dream?"

Then I shared my thinking. "'Why are the ornaments so tall?' makes me think about the big goals this girl might reach if she's willing to stretch high enough. My question about jeweled moments seems easy now that I've thought about the poem. I think 'jewels' are precious moments in her life. But I think there's more to reaching the ornaments than lifting her arms."

I switched marker colors to illustrate questions stemming from questions. "So now I'm wondering about the word 'if.' It says *if* she can stretch high enough to claim them. Does this mean she might not be able to reach high enough to claim those moments? What would be holding her back? Is she successful in the end? How can I stretch to my fullest and reach my life goals? Is stretching higher a way of saying work hard, go the extra mile?

"Poets often leave us messages," I told the kids, "but want us to figure out what those messages are. With poetry, it's fun to read the lines, think about our questions and answers, and then come up with our own idea about what the poem means. My questions today led me to this message: It's important to keep reaching for goals, because if we are successful, the rewards become the highlights of our life."

The students were ready to have a go at poetry themselves.

I told them, "On your desks, you'll find two poems waiting for you. All the poems in the room are different. First, decide which poem you want to focus on; then write your questions in the margin."

"You mean leave them in the snow?" Benton asked.

"Exactly. Then review your questions to see if you can figure out the meaning. You're ready. It's reading time."

Later, during the share session, children sat in groups of four around the room, knee to knee and eye to eye. They read the poems they'd chosen to their discussion groups, shared several questions they raised, and talked about the poems' messages. Through their questioning, the students figured out some very sophisticated poetry on their own.

Questions to Reveal Thinking

Here are some questions to help uncover how questioning is working with your students:

- Did you have a question even before you started to read this book?

- How is asking questions working for you? How do you plan to keep track of your questions? How does that question affect your understanding of this story?

- Wait a minute! When you read that line, it made me stop and think. Let me read it back to you. What's your question when you hear these words?

- Do you have a question following you through the book? Great! So why is it important to ask questions as you read?

- What questions do you have now that you've reread this poem? How did rereading change your questions? What do you notice about these new questions? What have you learned about the power of rereading?

- Do you notice yourself asking questions when your reading doesn't make sense? Oh, you've stopped to ask a question about the meaning of this word. Is that word keeping you from understanding? How will you figure out its meaning?

- Do you have any questions you expect the author to answer? Which one is the most important for you as a reader? Will you keep it in mind as you read further today? Here's a sticky note. If the author answers that question, or if you're given surprise information, mark that spot with a sticky. I can't wait to find out what happens.

- Did you notice the author just asked a question? What does that say to us as readers? Yes, they do that so we'll pay attention. It's a great device to use as an author. You might like to try asking questions in your writing as well.

- You've just finished reading this chapter. Which questions are still unanswered? How will thinking about those leftover questions help you dig in to the meaning of the next part of the book?

- Think about this question you've written in the margin. What else does it make you wonder about? Do you see what you just did as a reader? The first question made you stop and think about a deeper question. What new ideas come to you now about the meaning of this news article?

- Good for you! Your brain was watching for the answer to your earlier question, and here it is. It makes sense to take out that sticky note now that you've found the answer. You've covered a lot of new information and built your background knowledge. Researchers often need to stop and think about what it is they need to know to continue. Our questions change as we understand more about a topic. Take some time now to generate new questions to push you further in your research project.

- As I listen to you talk about your questions, I notice you keep coming back to this one in particular. You say the text doesn't answer it for you. When we ask questions not answered in our reading, it causes us to add our thinking to the story. What's your thinking about the answer to this question? Are there clues in the text to help you with your answer?

- Now that you've finished the story, do you have any new questions? When I finish a book, my lingering questions often send me back to reread. I'll be checking with you to find out what answers you've discovered after you reread today.

- What advice would you give someone outside our class about how asking questions helps you better understand what you read?

Teachers and Parents Together

- Have students keep track of all the questions they ask over the weekend. Compile the questions to generate a huge hall chart to hang in the main entrance for all to read.

- Interview parents to find out how they use questions at work. How do landscape architects, chefs, accountants, and moms and dads use questions to be successful at their jobs?

- Have a parent and child come up with a burning question. For instance, "Why are there so many different kinds of wildflowers?" From the questions generated, create "We wonder" books. These questions just might launch independent research projects.

CHAPTER 5

Weaving Sense into Words

KEY 4: DRAWING INFERENCES

When the mind is thinking, it is talking to itself.

—PLATO

T HIS CHAPTER FOCUSES on the reader's ability to expand
and deepen understanding by using inference to go beyond the
words on the page.

💡 **Enlighten Yourself First**

*Boori Ma, sweeper of the stairwell, had not slept in
two nights. So the morning before the third night she shook the
mites out of her bedding. She shook the quilts once underneath
the letter boxes where she lived, then once again at the mouth
of the alley, causing the crows who were feeding on vegetable
peels to scatter in several directions.*

*As she started up the four flights to the roof, Boori Ma kept
one hand placed over the knee that swelled at the start of every
rainy season. That meant that her bucket, quilts and the bundle of reeds which served as her broom all had to be braced*

---

under one arm. Lately Boori Ma had been thinking that the stairs were getting steeper; climbing them felt more like climbing a ladder than a staircase. She was sixty-four years old, with hair in a knot no larger than a walnut, and she looked almost as narrow from the front as she did from the side.

—"A Real Durwan," *Interpreter of Maladies*,
Jhumpa Lahiri, page 70

Interpreter of Maladies, a short story collection by Jhumpa Lahiri, won the 2000 Pulitzer Prize for fiction. Each story gives a glimpse of either life in India or life as a first-generation American. As I read the first three stories, I realize that in this unfamiliar terrain I have to concentrate especially hard to understand. I also notice that part of Lahiri's art is density and brevity. I don't have the luxury of easing my way into each story. Every sentence counts, if I am to build meaning from Lahiri's words.

As I read the first paragraph of "A Real Durwan," I wonder why Boori Ma hasn't slept in two nights and guess it is because of the mites. I picture Boori Ma vigorously shaking her bedding and wonder why she doesn't wash the quilts to get rid of the pests. Perhaps she has no place to wash. Her living conditions are meager and unsanitary.

During one of my years of teaching at a private school in Denver, there was an outbreak of head lice. Memories of tossing out infected classroom cushions and of morning head checks remind me that anyone could suffer this problem!

Yet an unmistakable sense of poverty envelops this old woman, who lives under letter boxes, out of doors, unprotected from the elements. The alley is filled with garbage and scavenging crows. The story is set in India, and Boori Ma is homeless or close to it. I've collected these clues to draw inferences: the mention of a "rainy season," Boori Ma's name, how she lives, her makeshift broom "a bundle of reeds."

Boori Ma is the "sweeper of the stairwell," an oddly formal title for a minor custodial job, but one that lends Boori Ma some shred of dignity. She's held this post for a long time, long enough to feel that the stairs are growing steeper with her advancing age. "With hair in a knot no larger than a walnut" implies her hair is very thin. "She looked almost as narrow from the front as she did from the side." Clearly, she lives on the margin, with minimal food or life necessities.

What will happen to this aging "sweeper of the stairwell" with the swollen knee and the sleepless nights? At 64, living alone in such harsh conditions, she faces an uncertain future. I'm intrigued to find out more. I predict that her struggle to maintain her already precarious position will provide the energy to drive this story forward.

—Chryse

A LOOK INSIDE THE MIND

By using inference, you elaborate upon what you read, drawing conclusions, going beyond what is written on the page. The voice inside your head doesn't simply parrot back the author's words, but instead makes guesses, finds connecting points, asks questions. You predict what might happen next, see a scene more clearly in your mind, figure out an unknown word, answer questions. You personalize what you read to build a deeper meaning.

Chryse's fifth-grade teacher called it "reading between the lines." But that never seemed to help Chryse as she searched the white space, trying to uncover meaning and finding only blanks between the lines of print. Now she tells her own students that meaning is found between their ears, not between the lines. Inferring involves forming a best guess about what the "evidence" (words, sentences, and paragraphs) means; speculating about what's to come; and then drawing conclusions about what was read to deepen the meaning of the literal words on the page.

Chryse asked questions about the opening paragraphs of "The Real Durwan," then went on to answer them by blending her background knowledge with the words in the story. She used her background experience with head lice to help form an opinion about Boori Ma's living conditions. She made predictions about the struggles facing Boori Ma, then drew conclusions about her possible fate. Chryse envisioned the scene: the anxious quilt shaking, the creaky climb up the stairs, the rotting garbage. Her prediction about forthcoming struggles might prove wrong. She might need to adjust her inferences as she reads further. But for now, her predictions and conclusions have launched her into the story.

Cartoons As an Example of Inference

Cartoons provide excellent examples of the need to infer. There is a reason some cartoons make you laugh, while others go right over your head. Your funny bone is really your background experience combining with the cartoon's words and pictures to create that "got it" laugh.

A fifth grader in Andrea Harris's class in Hanover, New Hampshire, where Chryse was giving a demonstration lesson on inferring, confessed that he didn't *get* a Far Side cartoon showing a mountain goat on a hillside seen through the windshield of the cockpit. One pilot says to the other, "Say . . . What's a mountain goat doing way up here in a cloud bank?"

Martin had no trouble reading the caption. But the words had no meaning for him.

Chryse suggested, "Think about your own flying experience. What do you see as you look out the plane window? Can you picture a 'cloud bank'?"

A flash of understanding crossed his face. "They're going to crash!" he shouted, sending nods of approval through the classroom.

This 10-year-old almost missed the point of the cartoon. But by combining his background knowledge with the clues in the picture and caption, he was able to uncover the crux of the joke. He had learned the critical role of inferring.

PUTTING FORTH YOUR OWN INTERPRETATIONS

There are many children who can "word call" beautifully. They appear to read fluently, but they aren't touched by what they read and are indifferent about finishing a book. They rarely make predictions or relate to the characters. They rush through pages to check off homework assignments, but real understanding escapes them. For them the words are only sounds strung together. There's no meaning.

Other students are unable to create a personal interpretation of what they're reading. They sit through hours of class with the teacher directing them to uncover the *author's* meaning. They haven't been taught to trust their own interpretations.

So, how can you help your child learn to infer?

The first step is to encourage her to talk and think about her own response to what she reads. "What do you think?" is a good place to

start. "What struck you about this?" With a few simple questions and a receptive ear, you help her create a sense of ownership. When your daughter realizes the power she has to make sense of what she reads, she'll become hooked on reading.

The best reading gift you can give your child is to honor her thinking. You want her to feel she has a personal stake in finding the answers to her predictions. You want her to know her unique interpretations matter. This is what will make reading exciting, fun, and, ultimately, meaningful to her.

You can help your child understand that she makes inferences throughout the day, not just when she reads. In effect, everyone "reads" the world, taking in external clues, combining them with understanding of how the world works, and drawing conclusions based on a blend of evidence and personal experience.

A child can size up Dad's exhausted slouch in the recliner when he's fixated on Monday night football and infer it's not a good time to ask for more allowance. A 6-year-old guesses from her mom's expression that the toy she reached for at the checkout counter will not end up on the grocery bill. A boy hears his father on the phone and, while privy to only half the conversation, infers that soccer practice was cancelled.

Just as your child is becoming an expert at reading body language, picking up clues from a one-sided phone conversation, and making predictions about what will happen, she can also use similar skills to draw inferences from her reading.

DEMONSTRATE INFERENTIAL THINKING

When you read to your child, you can share the behind-the-scenes thinking needed to draw inferences.

Once, sandwiched between her young nephews Neale (9 years old) and Jacob (4) on a road trip from Denver to Omaha, Chryse read them a Clifford book. On each page, the huge red dog accidentally crashed into buildings, dump trucks, or light poles. She explained to the kids how Clifford's big body kept getting him into different mishaps, until her sister Laura interjected, "They really leave a lot out of the story. You have to make up Clifford's disasters in your mind."

Chryse, then, consciously went beyond the words in the book and encouraged her nephews to talk about each of Clifford's funny encounters. At one point Neale piped up: "Oops! Clifford's not supposed to play with the electrical spools. He thinks they're a toy. I bet he gets in trouble!"

Sure enough, on the next page Clifford crashed the heavy spool through a neighbor's garage. Neale's prediction helped him understand the worried look on the dog's face as he watched the spool's path of destruction. Without thinking back to the words and the pictures, Neale would have missed the humor surrounding the gangly dog's mishaps.

Word Games Build the Power to Infer

Word games also help children develop their ability to infer. The road trip progressed with Chryse and Laura switching among reading to the boys, driving, and playing diversionary games.

One of the boys' favorite games was the Simile Game. One person would call out a phrase like, "As prickly as a _____." Then they would rotate around the car, taking turns to fill in the blank. The tricky part was not to repeat a previous guess. As the miles ticked away, they identified what was sticky, scary, tiny, grouchy, and so on. Jacob and Neale took in the clues, added their background knowledge, and inferred a word. They gained insight into inferential thinking as they completed the puzzle.

They also played Twenty Questions. Three of them would try to guess the identity of a mystery person or thing by asking questions of the fourth person. The guessing group was allowed to ask a total of twenty questions. If they collectively failed to zero in on the identity, the person who launched the round got a point.

> Word games are a playful way to develop your child's inferential thinking and, ultimately, his reading ability.

"Is it a police officer?" Jacob queried.

"Does this person help people?" Laura asked. "Give us another clue!"

Slowly, they deduced the occupation or identity of the mystery thing or person.

Word games help children pay attention to clues, ask questions, connect their background experience to the evidence, make predictions, and confirm or revamp their guesses to win the game. Word games are a playful way to develop your child's inferential thinking and, ultimately, his reading ability.

Make Reading Come Alive

On the same interminable road trip, Chryse read Chris Van Allsburg's *Two Bad Ants*. A literal retelling of the story would simply describe two ants experiencing one harrowing adventure after another. But as they thought about the words and the pictures, Chryse's nephews realized there was more to the story. The ants' adventure was taking place in an everyday setting, a kitchen. The bitter water the ants were swirled in wasn't a storm at sea but a cup of coffee.

At one point the unsuspecting ants climb into a "hiding place."

"Oh, no!" yelled Jacob when he got it. "They're in a toaster!" His prediction was borne out when on the next page the ants were rocketed upward as the bread propelled their hot bodies "flying through the air."

As the story progressed, Neale blurted out, "I know where they are now! They're in a garbage disposal."

Chryse couldn't resist probing a bit. "What clues did you use to figure that out?"

Neale reread the sentence: "The ants were caught in a whirling storm of shredded food and stinging rain. Listen to the words and look at the picture. When we turn on *our* disposal, it cuts up the food and the water rushes around inside. It's *got* to be the disposal!"

INFERRING UNKNOWN WORDS

Inference also helps unlock unknown words. A group of first graders listened to their teacher read *Abuela*, a fanciful tale of a young girl and her grandmother who fly together over Manhattan. Their brightly colored skirts billow in the wind as the pair turns somersaults in midair. The text is sprinkled with Spanish phrases.

Children with English-only backgrounds struggle when presented with the Spanish words. Sounding them out doesn't help them uncover the meaning. It has to be inferred.

> "*Cuidado*," Abuela would tell me. We'd have to be careful as we went for a short ride.
>
> —*ABUELA*, ARTHUR DORROS, PAGE 20

Mustering their evidence from a retelling of what had happened so far, as well as noting clues from the words and the pictures, the children put forth their best guess as to the meaning of *cuidado*.

"I think it means 'come,'" Arnie offered. "That word matches with the picture. See? The girl is doing handstands on the plane and wants her grandmother to come."

"No, I think it means 'be careful.' It makes more sense," Emily guessed as the kids pored over the words and the pictures. "On each page, the grandmother gives advice to the girl. I think she's telling her to be careful as they hang on to the plane for a short ride. She *better* be careful!"

And "careful" it is!

The children continued to infer the meaning of other phrases by using clues, visual evidence, and their understanding of the story and by thinking about what would make sense. The payoff came when two bilingual students burst forth with the right answers and the others could check their guesses.

When you're reading with your child, help him uncover unknown words by encouraging him to use his inferring skills. Show him that the clues to figuring out the mystery word are often in the picture and preceding sentences. Let him hear you reason through how you arrived at the word that makes the most sense. Make it fun, like solving a riddle. Every now and then, liven things up with an off-the-wall guess.

The Power of Predicting

Judy Galbraith, author of *You Know Your Child is Gifted When . . . A Beginner's Guide to Life on the Bright Side*, suggests that the difference between the bright child and the gifted child is that the bright child is good at memorizing, while the gifted child is good at guessing. What better gift to give *your* child than to model how to guess what's to come in a story, then sit back and watch him take over this simple but critical concept himself!

The mere act of looking at a book's title and cover raises questions about what's to come. From your predictions based on clues gathered from this piece of evidence, you prepare to uncover new ideas, answer questions, follow an adventure, and meet new characters.

The cover of *The Raft*, by Jim LaMarche, shows a shirtless boy poling his raft down a river. It appears to be a lazy summer day. The boy smiles over his shoulder while a raccoon ripples the water with

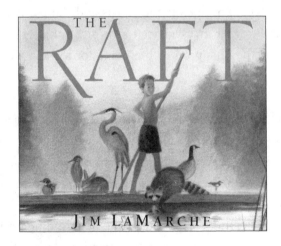

one paw and a heron keeps watch by the boy's side. It's a safe bet you won't be reading about life in a crowded city!

A conversation with your child about *The Raft*'s cover might sound like this: "It looks like this boy is having loads of fun floating down the river. But I'm surprised all these birds and animals are making the trip with him. They all look so peaceful. I think this book will be about all that happens on the raft trip with the boy and the animals. What do you guess?"

The child who predicts before reading has a stake in what's to come. He wants to see if his guess is correct. It's fine if it isn't. The point is to be connected enough to what he is reading to make a thoughtful prediction and to *want* to find out if he is right.

As the book progresses, you and your child might have to revise some thinking and amend some guesses. In *The Raft*, it turns out Nicky is forced to spend the summer with his grandmother, far from friends and a television. The smile depicted on the cover comes only after he discovers an old raft floating near his grandmother's house. And the animals come later.

> It wasn't just birds that the raft attracted. One morning three raccoons followed me along the shore. Another time a turtle climbed on board and spent the morning sunning itself. And one afternoon I saw a family of foxes slip through the trees along the river.
>
> —*THE RAFT*, JIM LAMARCHE, PAGE 15

You can call your child's attention to Nicky's special powers when he's on the raft. "Let's go back to look at the cover. Does it seem strange that all these animals get along so well? From the way the story's going and the cover, I bet he'll meet even more animals as he spends time on the raft. What do you think?"

Your child will confirm or dismiss old predictions and make new ones as he reads. He'll elaborate on ideas not directly stated by the author. Through educated guesses about what is yet to come, he'll begin to draw conclusions about larger ideas in the story and keep turning the pages, because he *wants* to.

FIGURE OUT THE BIG MESSAGE

Writers give clues, but readers have to amass the evidence and draw conclusions for themselves. Often the deepest meanings from a book or story go well beyond what's literally stated. Call them life lessons, new insights, the moral of the story. Finding these larger truths is one of the reasons people read. Kids need the challenge of thinking hard and experiencing their own "aha"s.

Parents can help by getting books that engage their children in interesting ideas. Take Allen Say's *The Sign Painter*. In the first part, readers meet a young artist whose real love is painting landscapes. He takes a job painting a series of billboards in the desert. Each is to be the same: He's to paint a huge face of a blonde woman accompanied by the word "ArrowStar."

> Writers give clues, but readers have to amass the evidence and draw conclusions for themselves.

Your conversation about the story might sound like this: "Okay. So the young artist likes to paint landscapes, but he's got to do the same face over and over again. He's sure not doing what he loves. He just goes from billboard to billboard, doing the same old thing. His heart isn't in the job. It makes me think about your uncle Fred. He hated his job, but kept plugging away year after year. Do you think the artist will continue painting something he cares so little about? Do you think he should give up on the idea of being a real painter because he needs to earn a living?"

You might talk about what it's like to follow your dreams and what the consequences of life choices might mean. Let your child hear your thoughts. Ponder various possibilities. Show how your understanding evolves as you gather clues from the turn of events. Model for your child how you make inferences as the characters move through the story.

What Kids Say

Inferring

- "It helps you concentrate on your book more."

- "It helps me understand the humor, and that helps me understand how characters are feeling. I'm part of the book."

- "It slows me down, and I think harder."

- "Predictions help me pay attention to see if it really happens."

- "It helps me read with feeling."

—FROM SHARON MESSENGER'S FIRST-GRADE CLASS

- "An inference is when you spill your thinking on the book."

- "When you read, your brain is like the pushmi-pullyu in Doctor Dolittle's book. One side takes in the words, and the other side thinks about them!"

—FROM BARB SMITH'S SECOND-GRADE CLASS

- "An inference is when you take the important words and turn them into thoughts. They get trapped in your head, making you stop and think about ideas the author hasn't quite told you."

- "I'm inferring when I get the feeling of something going on in the book, but the author hasn't really told me in the words."

- "An inference is the opposite of a reference because a reference is a source right in front of you, and an inference is information you have to put together yourself."

—FROM THIRD, FOURTH, AND FIFTH GRADERS

Books That Require Inferring

Picture Books

Sachiko Means Happiness, Kimiko Sakai

Floss, Kim Lewis

The Day of Ahmed's Secret, Florence Parry Heide and
  Judith Heide Gilliland

The Royal Bee, Frances and Ginger Park

The Other Side, Jacqueline Woodson

An Angel for Solomon Singer, Cynthia Rylant

Longer Books

Poppy, Avi (160 pages)

Out of the Dust, Karen Hesse (227 pages)

Holes, Louis Sachar (233 pages)

A Wrinkle in Time, Madeleine L'Engle (211 pages)

The Lost Years of Merlin, T. A. Barron (367 pages)

Once your child starts making inferences, she'll be making the book her own. She'll be engaged and excited by the meaning books hold.

TIPS FOR PARENTS: ENCOURAGING INFERENCE

Inferring has long been considered a "higher" thinking skill. Supposedly, only older kids need apply. Time and again, however, teachers find that young children are fully capable of making inferences as they listen to stories. Your young child can experience the fun of guessing

Language for Drawing Inferences

"I predict . . ."

"I think that . . ."

"My guess is . . ."

"That's just what I thought . . ."

"Now, this is a surprise . . ."

"My conclusion here is . . ."

what the next page will hold. He'll be an engaged listener when he's able to put in his two cents' worth. The fact is children of all ages *need* to infer.

Talking with your child about everyday life is the cornerstone for his future success in inferential thinking. Share the thinking behind your decisions. Be willing to admit you're not sure about something, but explain what your thinking is so far. A conversation like "Look at those dark clouds. I'm guessing we're going to get some rain this afternoon" or "I'm going to stop reading for a minute so we can think together about what this all means" will help your child develop his ability to think and infer.

For Preschool Readers

Playing word games, reading riddle books, and listening to rhyming songs are fun ways to set the stage for inferring. "I'm thinking of something that is red and begins with an A."

"Can you eat it?"

"Yes!" you say.

"Is it an apple?"

"You got it!"

This simple exchange holds all the components of inferring. The child takes the clues from the riddle, connects them to his background knowledge about the alphabet and what he know about apples, thinks about what would make sense, and predicts an answer.

Leaving off the rhyming word in a poem or song provides the same sort of experience. "Humpty Dumpty sat on a wall. Humpty Dumpty had a great _____." Here, prior knowledge of the nursery rhyme or knowledge of what would rhyme with "wall" helps your child successfully predict what would fit in the phrase. You'll have fun guessing and predicting together, and you'll be teaching your youngster to infer at the same time.

When you infer, you take a chance. Putting forth a guess, coming up with an idea, and making a prediction can be scary business. What a great opportunity it is for you to foster this skill in a loving environment where it's okay to be wrong, where you can hug when you solve the riddle and shrug when you miss a telling clue.

Cuddle up with your 5-year-old with a book like Pat Upton's *Who Does This Job?* The first page asks, "Who grows this corn?"

You might say, "I'm going to search for answers. Look—here are the clues. I see cows walking through a cornfield and a barn in this corner. I know a farmer has all of these things. I think a farmer grows the corn. That's my prediction." On the next page the farmer fesses up.

Letting your child hear how you came up with the answer will show him how to create inferences. Soon he'll copy your lead and make inferences on his own.

For Emerging Readers

You can help your child shape an idea about a character by reflecting on how the character acts at the beginning of the story and changes by the end. Avoid the "grill and kill" book discussions many of us remember from our school days. Instead, share ideas on an equal footing with your child. You can show her the thinking behind your conclusions, but you need to leave the door open for a true exchange of ideas. When kids know you are really curious about their thinking, they come up with amazing insights.

In Julie Brinckloe's *Fireflies!* you are introduced to a boy who catches a glimpse of the first firefly leaving its lit pattern in the evening dusk. His excited rush through dinner is inferred when he says: "I forked the meat and corn and potatoes into my mouth. 'Please, may I go out? The fireflies. . . .'"

You might say, "This kid really loves catching fireflies! He rushed to the basement to find a jar and ran outside to be the first to capture some. I can almost feel his excitement when he says: 'I felt a tremble of joy and shouted, "I can catch hundreds!"'"

Your child might add, "I bet he'll fill the whole jar. Look how he's dancing around with that big smile."

This sort of dialogue fills out the main character. You note his actions, hear him shout to his friends, and, by the end of the evening, proudly report to his dad about his full jar of fireflies.

But the boy's mood changes when he notices the light in the jar dimming. "They were *my* fireflies. I caught them. They made moonlight in my jar."

Because you understood the boy's pride and his passion for capturing fireflies, you can infer the dilemma he faces when he needs to make a decision about the insects' fate. The boy has progressed from a carefree romp with his friends to this poignant conclusion:

> I held the jar, dark and empty, in my hands. The moonlight and the fireflies swam in my tears, but I could feel myself smiling.
>
> —*Fireflies!*, Julie Brinckloe, page 28

You can commiserate with him as he frees his prized collection. It *is* often hard to do the right thing. That's an inference, and an important one.

For Advancing Readers

Louis Sachar's Newbery Medal winner *Holes* grips the reader right away. Stanley Yelnats (his first name is his last name spelled backward) has been unjustly accused of committing a crime and is sent to Camp Green Lake, a boot camp for delinquent boys that's situated in a dried-up lake bed in the heart of a Texas desert.

After arriving at the juvenile correctional facility, Stanley is stripped of his clothes, issued the standard orange suit, and given his instructions from Mr. Sir: "You are to dig one hole each day, including Saturdays and Sundays. Each hole must be five feet deep, and five feet across in every direction. Your shovel is your measuring stick. Breakfast is served at 4:30. . . . This isn't a Girl Scout camp."

Based on the circumstances presented so far, you infer this camp is a long way from a lighthearted marshmallow roast around a campfire. You guess Mr. Sir is warning Stanley about what is to come. You might say, "I'm thinking this hole digging is really harsh punishment for these kids. What do you think will happen next?"

You and your child quickly discover there's more to the story than poor Stanley's daily dig in the dry lake bed. A parallel plot emerges about the inhabitants of this once thriving community, specifically a robber named Kissin' Kate Barlow. You both sense that the mean warden's passion for hole digging has more to do with greedy self-interest than with instilling character in the juveniles.

Holes becomes even more absorbing as you and your child dig through the facts, adding your questions, predictions, connections, and visual images to what's going on. At one point, you wonder why the deadly yellow-spotted lizard fails to bite both Stanley and his buddy, Zero, as they uncover the treasure situated in the midst of the lizards' nest.

"It was amazing how those lizards crawled all over the boys and finally left them alone so they could get out of the hole with the box! I'm remembering the advice Sam gave the folks of Green Lake many years ago. Remember he thought onions could cure a person of just about any ailment?"

Your child might add her thinking. "Wait a minute—to keep up their strength, the boys ate all those onions! And lizards hate onions. That's what saved them!"

Sachar himself asks his readers to come up with their own discoveries. He writes:

> But it would be boring to go through all the tedious details of all the changes in their lives. Instead, the reader will be presented with one last scene, which took place almost a year and a half after Stanley and Hector left Camp Green Lake.
>
> You will have to fill in the holes yourself.
>
> —*HOLES*, LOUIS SACHAR, PAGE 231

As you and your child fit the pieces together, a clear picture of the present-day characters and their ancestors emerges. By inferring, you've made sense of a complicated situation.

 ## CLASSROOM CONNECTIONS: DRAWING INFERENCES

> *In her classroom our speculations ranged the world. She breathed curiosity into us, so that each morning we came to her carrying new truths, new facts, new ideas, cupped and sheltered in our hands like captured fireflies. When she went away a sadness came over us. But the light did not go out. She had written her signature upon us: the literature of the teacher who writes on children's minds. Many teachers have taught me soon forgotten things, but only a few like her created in me a new direction, a new hunger, a new attitude. I suppose that to a large extent I am the unsigned manuscript of that teacher. What deathless power lies in the hands of such a person.*
>
> —*A Former Teacher,* John Steinbeck

If teachers want classrooms where "our speculations ranged the world," if they want kids who come carrying "new truths, new facts, new ideas," they must teach students the power of inferring.

Crafting Session

How might teachers launch a strategy study on inferring? A compelling picture book, a provocative newspaper article, a short chapter from a novel, or a page from *Ranger Rick* magazine can all be sources to model our thinking and begin to build a collective definition of what it means to infer. Chryse describes below how she teaches inferring to a class of sixth graders.

On the kickoff day of inferring, I used to rush into the classroom, waving my definition proudly printed on a poster: TEXT + BACKGROUND KNOWLEDGE = AN AHA. The students would listen respectfully as I further elaborated on the meaning, but they clearly didn't grasp what this meant for them as readers. I needed to *show* them how to infer.

One day, I decided to take a chance by modeling how I thought through a *Peanuts* cartoon strip, warning the class that I'm not good at reading cartoons. "You're better at it than I am," I told the class. "Your job is to tell me what you saw me doing as a reader after I'm done."

Taped to large chart paper were four enlarged sections of Charles Schulz's cartoon. "So, I'm noticing in this first panel that these two characters are outside. I see a tree, grass, and the corner of a building. I'm not sure if they are boys or girls. They look like they're walking. I picture them chatting together on a sunny day. I think this one is a girl. She's carrying a large envelope very carefully. She has a smile on her face and says, 'Snoopy typed my term paper for me.'

"Those words make me a little nervous. I know Snoopy is a dog. How smart is it to give a dog control over something as important as a term paper? I used to work on term papers for weeks. I hope she rereads it before turning it in."

Crafting Session Tips

- An inference elaborates on what you read as you draw conclusions that go beyond what is on the page.

- Create an inference by connecting your background knowledge with the clues in the text or pictures to form an opinion about what is not clearly stated.

- An inference can be the answer to a question raised as the story is read.

- A sensory image is an inference in picture form.

- Inferring involves thinking ahead about what could happen next. You make predictions and then confirm or reject them.

- You infer when you make educated guesses about what's going on in your reading.

- Infer the meaning of unknown words by using the context of the sentence and the clues in the picture to figure out what would make the most sense.

- An inference is a personal discovery about what the author didn't quite specifically write.

- Feeling empathy for characters, laughing at a joke, discovering an answer to a riddle, getting a sense about the setting of a story, reacting to facts, and solving a mystery are all part of inferential thinking.

I talked about the words, the accompanying drawings, and what was going on in my mind. I jotted down my thinking on the chart paper as I shared the thoughts out loud.

I continued writing and reasoning through the next three panels. By the time I finished, the white chart paper was a blur of questions and connections about what went on in my mind.

I wanted to show the students my explicit thinking so they could understand how to make inferences in their own reading, be it a Far Side cartoon, a newspaper editorial, or a complex chapter in a novel.

In response to my notes and actions, the students came up with the following list about what it means to infer:

- Stopping to think and rereading
- Connecting what you know to the words and pictures
- Recapping what has happened so far
- Asking a question about what could happen next
- Paying attention to the details in the drawings
- Thinking back about what the words could mean
- Talking to yourself and then stating an opinion
- Trying to see it in your mind
- Combining clues left by the author
- Coming up with a conclusion, guess, or bigger idea

This list certainly meant more to the students than my definition! In the weeks that followed, they applied to their own reading what they had seen me doing.

Questions to Reveal Thinking

Here are some suggestions to use to uncover your students' inferential thinking after you've modeled the concept in crafting sessions:

- The author gives you a gift in the title. Before you read, what prediction popped into your head? How did having this prediction help you as a reader?
- Now that you're almost finished with this chapter, have you confirmed your earlier prediction? What did it sound like in your head when you found the answer? Can you share with the class how our predictions sometimes come out completely differently from what we suspected?

- This is a tricky word. What word would make sense here? How did you infer its meaning from its place in this sentence?

- We need to not only pay attention to what the words say but also work to create new meaning. How is this new way of thinking helping you better understand your reading?

- Authors leave clues for us as we read. Our job is to put them together to figure out big ideas. Has this happened to you today? Great! You might like to take these sticky notes and re-trace your thinking to mark some of the clues you uncovered as you first read this chapter.

- Good for you! You've just done a great retelling of this story. Please write this new insight in your response journal today.

- What message do you think the author wanted you to understand? How did you come up with this new thinking? How will this help you remember your reading?

- When you go over these facts for your report, what do they all mean to you?

- How did you determine there was a change in time? What words brought you to that conclusion? As a writer, how will you use this idea of revealing what's going on, not coming right out and telling the reader? What does it mean to write so your reader can infer?

- How would you explain how to infer to someone outside our class? How does inferring help you see and understand what you read?

Teachers and Parents Together

- Have a small group of parents model for the class a book talk about a provocative picture book. Seat the students in a circle around the parents to notice what happens in an informal book club discussion. This is a great launch for forming class book clubs, providing kids with an opportunity to hear a variety of inferential thinking on the same book. (This suggestion is from our friend Debbie Miller, a brilliant teacher and the author of *Reading with Meaning*.)

- For homework, have students write poems and riddles for their parents to infer meaning, and ask the parents to leave their thinking in the margins.

- Invite parents in for a celebration of inferring. Read student-generated riddles and poetry; play charades; guess the use of unusual kitchen items; figure out the mystery substances in bottles; share examples of well-crafted descriptive pieces; read and solve mysteries together; sketch and write the endings to a thrilling story.

CHAPTER 6

What's Important and Why

KEY 5: DETERMINING IMPORTANCE

KEY 6: SYNTHESIZING

I know of nothing more inspiring than that of making discoveries for one's self.

—George Washington Carver

THIS CHAPTER FOCUSES on two skills: the ability to distinguish what's important in text and the ability to synthesize it, or determine the overall meaning and significance.

Enlighten Yourself First

These are the two poles I want to travel between in these pages: my boyish view of the pointlessness of flowers and the unreasonable passion for them that the Dutch briefly epitomized. The boy's-eye view has the wintry weight of rationality on its side: all this useless beauty is impossible to justify on cost–benefit grounds. But then, isn't that always how it is with beauty? Overboard as the Dutch would eventually go, the fact is that the rest of us— that is, most of humankind for most of its history—have been in the same irrational boat as the seventeenth-century Dutch: crazy for flowers.

So what is this tropism all about, for us and for the flowers? How did these organs of plant sex manage to get themselves cross-wired with human ideas of value and status and Eros? And what might our ancient attraction for flowers have to teach us about the deeper mysteries of beauty—what one poet has called "this grace wholly gratuitous"? Is that what it is? Or does beauty have a purpose?

—"The Tulip," *The Botany of Desire: A Plant's-Eye View of the World*, Michael Pollan, page 64

Judy, our project manager at the Public Education and Business Coalition, knew I'd dive into Pollan's book the minute it was pulled from the package. *The Botany of Desire* was clearly right for me, a gardening fanatic. Judy wanted me to decide if we should use it as a reading choice at an upcoming workshop.

Each paragraph in this chapter, "The Tulip," is dense with information. Pen in hand, I read and jot down notes in the margins, keeping track of my thinking. The chapter is arranged in unnamed sections, each marked off by extra space, a line, and dots. I expect that each section will contain distinct information and that the format will help organize the material into manageable chunks.

Pollan begins, "These are the two poles I want to travel between in these pages."

I wonder what the poles will be, if they will be the primary focus of the chapter. To describe the first, his "boyish view" of flowers, he uses the words "unreasonable," "pointless," "irrational," "useless." Those words jar me. My passion for growing cutting flowers led me to rip out an old swimming pool in our yard to create even more space for beds. I can't conceive of anyone describing flowers in such negative terms. I think, Pollan's got it all wrong.

Sifting through the paragraph, though, I find the other "pole" he plans to travel. It has to do with the beauty of flowers. Not only the 17th-century Dutch but "most of humankind for most of its history" has been "crazy for flowers." Here, Pollan has me pegged: I've been known to visit my plots in the dead of night, flashlight in hand, impatiently checking the status of available blossoms to cut for waiting arrangements.

Now I understand Pollan's internal debate, the "two poles" he is traversing: "pointless beauty" versus "the deeper mystery of beauty." But I sense he's talking about more than flowers. What happened in 17th-century Holland took the obsession with ephemeral beauty to absurd extremes. It was called "tulipmania." Tulip connoisseurs paid a king's ransom for a single bulb, and the whole Dutch economy rose and fell on the market for these beautiful—but ultimately "useless"—commodities. What is the deeper meaning, "the unreasonable passion," that flowers embody? Does beauty have a purpose? Are there some things that can't be justified on cost–benefit grounds, but don't need to be?

I call Judy. "I learned a lot about tulips."

"So did I," she responds. "What struck me is that the bulbs the Dutch most prized were infected by a virus that caused the mutated stripe in their petals. They were actually defective!"

What the Dutch could not have known, I learn later in the book, was that a virus was responsible for the magic of the broken tulip, a fact that, as soon as it was discovered, doomed the beauty it had made possible.

"So what they saw as beautiful was really an abnormality. . . ." My voice trails off.

"Yes! I read another article about how variegated leaves are actually diseased. Over time, they 'heal' themselves to a more uniform green."

"That's exactly what's happening to my variegated Heliopsis," I blurt out. "I bought it for the white leaves with green veins, but the leaf is losing its definition. Now I under-stand why."

We laugh. Judy goes on. "In the scheme of things, I think Pollan was talking about a culture's perception of beauty, how subjective that is, and how our human choices contribute to the selection of what will survive." Judy has determined what is most important to her (the virus's impact on the bulbs) and synthesized that information to develop a larger insight about human society.

I'm still working on my own, very different synthesis. Is Pollan pointing out how fragile flowers are, how short-lived their beauty is? Is that part of the reason we become "crazy for flowers" as they open their blossoms to our gaze? Is their transient beauty a metaphor for our own fleeting lives? Do they have something deeper to teach us about the mysteries of beauty and of life itself? Is that why, in Pollan's words, they exert an "ancient attraction" over us?

—Chryse

THE ROLE OF DETERMINING IMPORTANCE

Turn on CNN and you'll be bombarded with information. In the lower left, weather forecasts from around the country are displayed, changing in seconds from Salt Lake City to Oakland to New York. Ticker tape news headlines scroll across the bottom of the screen. In the bottom right are continually changing market quotes and, next to them, individual stock prices. A newscaster talks about sniper attacks in the Washington, D.C., area, while photographs of crime scenes are displayed to her immediate left. Sports scores from the weekend's games start flashing across the bottom of the screen. What to watch? What to pay attention to? How to determine what's important?

The modern world is inundated by "facts." Television, the Inter-net—more information than your grandparents ever imagined—is at your fingertips with the click of a button. But there's a big difference between information and knowledge. As a friend of Susan's once said, "We have an abundance of information, but information alone is meaningless. It has to be thought about and organized and then internalized, and then maybe you will end up with knowledge."

You get from disparate facts to knowledge only if you take the time to determine what is important and synthesize that information so that it becomes meaningful. In reading and in life, you need to hone your skills of discriminating between what is important and what is not.

THE PROCESS OF DETERMINING IMPORTANCE

Things were simpler for students when all they had to do was find the main idea in their school reading. In text written just for this purpose, they would lift out the opening sentence or the concluding statement to identify the essence of each paragraph. They thought that was all there was to it. But most nonfiction is not arranged in this considerate, if boring, fashion. A critical part of comprehension is the ability to separate the nonessential from the essential.

When Chryse started the tulip chapter, she had a specific purpose: to decide whether the book should be one of the choices for the workshop. She then had to decide which part to read first. Choosing the tulip chapter, she read it with an eye toward identifying what was important, intriguing, and provocative in this potential reading choice. Pen in hand, she kept track of her thinking in the margins so she could review the information she found most critical.

She also made a special effort to pay attention to the layout. That helped her know when new information was being introduced. Her extensive background knowledge about gardening and her passion for flowers shored up her understanding of the concepts the author raised. She posed questions, flagged important information, and discussed the chapter with Judy.

Through this process, she determined what was important from the text and went beyond that to form her own conclusions about the overriding concept of the chapter. By using her background knowledge, asking questions, and making inferences, she synthesized the piece, gaining a deeper personal insight into the "purpose of beauty" while recognizing that Judy got something different, but equally profound, from the book. Clearly, this book would be a good choice for the workshop.

What Is Important?

Have you ever asked a friend for a recommendation of a good book to read, only to have the proposed book ruined as every detail was shared? Your friend didn't give you an overview but went meandering down side streets. Every detail seemed equally pertinent. She needed help determining what was important.

Determining importance has to do with knowing why you're reading and then making decisions about which information or ideas are most critical to understanding the overall meaning of the piece.

In your everyday life, you continually determine what's important, setting priorities, making decisions about what must be done now and what can wait. Imagine the furnace fails to click on, on that first crisp fall morning. You call the repairman. While he's checking things out, you wait for the verdict but also think about the 12-year-old car with 160,000 miles, the roof that needs some work, the state of your savings account. The furnace repairman says you might make it through another winter with the existing furnace, but he can't make any guarantees. You weigh the cost of a new unit versus the time and labor for the replacement parts. Setting priorities in your mind, determining what's important right here right now, you decide to hang on to the relic for yet another season.

> In your everyday life, you continually determine what's important, setting priorities, making decisions about what must be done now and what can wait.

The ability to figure out what's most important in text starts with several simple actions you should take *before* reading: deciding your purpose for reading; consciously searching for new facts; reading with specific questions in mind; and understanding that layout, particularly in nonfiction text, gives valuable clues to what's important. Even young children can understand how to integrate these steps into their everyday reading lives. When in place, these steps are powerful tools for determining what's important.

Why Are You Reading?

Knowing your purpose for reading helps determine what's important. You might read to escape, to laugh, to learn, to pursue passions, to answer gnawing questions, to get ready for a presentation, to finish a homework assignment.

Reading *Better Homes and Gardens* magazine in the supermarket checkout line is very different from reading the next novel for your book group. Leafing through the magazine pages, you might note before and after shots of kitchens and bathrooms and get some ideas for that next renovation. You might even take away a good recipe, but you're passing the time, not consciously pulling out key information.

Your book club novel is different. Not only do you want to remember the plot, characters, and sequence of events, but you also want to mull it all around in your head so you can contribute to the conversation. Your purpose for reading affects how carefully you read and has an impact on what you determine is important.

Looking for New Facts

A third-grade class reads Seymour Simon's *Animals Nobody Loves.* The teacher starts off saying, "This book always teaches me something I didn't know before. Remember when we learned all those things about the devil ray? They can be more than 20 feet across! Let's be on the lookout for amazing new facts."

During the day's reading, the class finds out that "cockroaches . . . can run as fast as 3 miles an hour, and a young roach can fit through a crack as thin as a dime."

In response to this new information, the teacher exclaims, "Yikes! They're fast and they can squeeze through almost any wall space. Maybe that's why it's so hard to get rid of them!"

This type of conversation helps the students articulate their purpose for reading and puts them on the lookout for additional catchy facts.

Eight-year-old Michael, an insect aficionado, flags a section explaining that a balloon spider had been spotted two miles up in the air.

"That really is amazing!" His teacher agrees. "How did you decide to mark that spot to remember?"

"Well, I'm a Cub Scout. Once we went on a 6-mile hike, and after two miles, I was *exhausted*. So I know how far two miles is and how amazing it is that balloon spiders have been found that far from the ground! Seems pretty important to me."

Michael had sifted through countless facts about insects, activated his background knowledge about the length of a six-mile hike, and then noticed when he was learning new information about the balloon spider. Being aware of adding new information to his mental files helped direct his search for what was important.

Seeking Answers to Questions

Another reason for reading is that you have a question driving your search. Your family may like snowshoeing in the mountains. Every year there are avalanche warnings and, tragically, fatalities. This raises a serious issue about investing in a rescue beacon. But you have questions: How do these things work? Do they really save lives in case of an avalanche? Are they worth $400?

With your child enlisted to help, you turn to Stephen Kramer's *Avalanche* for answers. The book has diagrams of how an avalanche starts and includes maps of areas with the greatest avalanche danger.

But you have a specific focus: You want to know about the effectiveness of beacons, so you quickly turn to the chapter titled "Rescue":

> Rescue work can be made faster and easier if everyone who goes into a snowy mountain area wears safety equipment. The best piece of equipment is a rescue beacon. . . .
>
> Everybody should turn the beacon on before they start to ski, snowmobile, or snowshoe. Then if a snowslide sweeps someone away, the other people in the group can turn on their beacons to pick up the lost person's signal. Within minutes, by walking back and forth over the snow and listening carefully, the group members can usually find the place where the person is buried.
>
> —*Avalanche*, Stephen Kramer, page 39

You tell your child, "Well, this answers our questions. Seems like a great investment to me."

In return he might say, "Mom, I think this tells us always to snowshoe with other folks who *also* have rescue beacons!"

Determining What Is Important

Your child reads an article about ptarmigans in *Falcon Magazine for Kids*. She reads three opening questions in varying sizes of bold print. She notes there is writing on four photographs of ptarmigans. She sees that the article is divided by five boldfaced headings. After reading the last photo caption, she looks at the title, which she'd skipped over at first. The first word of the title, "Magic," is in white-block letters barely detectable in a light gray background. The second word is "Show," which is partly obscured by a white bird, which in turn completely blends into the full-page spread. Without having read a word of the article, she uses the text structure to determine what is important to understand: Ptarmigans have incredible camouflage ability and can actually blend into the snow.

Your child figured out the value of layout. In much nonfiction writing, including textbooks, the layout provides critical tips for identifying what is important. Titles, bold headings, pictures with captions, quotations, timelines, graphs, and maps give valuable information about what's important. Help your child to preread factual material by paying attention to all of these hints. Text features are road signs for the reader. They point to what's important.

> Titles, bold headings, pictures with captions, quotations, timelines, graphs, and maps give valuable information about what's important.

Also, explore with your child the way nonfiction books are organized. When he begins to use text features to uncover information, he'll more easily glean what's important. In the book *Mount St. Helens National Volcanic Monument*, by Sharlene and Ted Nelson, there's a contents page listing the chapters, each dealing with a different aspect of the 1980 eruption of Mount St. Helens. Point out that in many fact-filled books the chapters don't need to be read in order. Ask if a particular chapter title piques his interest. Does he want to look at the pictures first and then choose? Often the pictures will generate a question or set your son on a quest for specific information that will help direct his reading.

Each page in this book has a photograph with a caption depicting a different aspect of the mountain. Note that pictures often reflect the most important information on a page, and the caption further highlights it. Without focusing on the table of contents, the pictures, and the captions, your child might miss an opportunity to get a leg up on what's going on.

When reading nonfiction books, don't let your child read too far without finding the glossary of important words (if there is one). These key words explain the essential concepts and vocabulary of the book and can help keep kids who are stumped by the unfamiliar words from giving up.

Indexes, too, come in handy. You want to build more background knowledge about the lava dome? Try pages 37 to 39. Knowing how to use an index will pay dividends in helping your child find specific information quickly.

FEED YOUR CHILD'S CURIOSITY

Chryse's family never passed up a historical marker on vacation. Their 1964 Pontiac station wagon would slow to a stop, and the three girls in the back knew what was coming. Dad cranked down the window, cleared his throat, and began to read about the Continental Divide, thermal pools, rock formations, Civil War battles, ghost towns. Each marker was photographed so it could be revisited at the end-of-summer family vacation slide show. Somehow, he made it all interesting and ignited in his children a curiosity to find out about places, people, and the world around them.

Curiosity drives people to uncover information important to them. Without a sense of wonder, without wanting to know more, people will find reading to be a dull and empty skill. A reader might go through the motions of uncovering the main idea, but curiosity propels the search and makes for an engaged detective who is able to identify clues and determine what's really important. By sharing interests, as Chryse's father did, you model a passion for learning that will help unleash your child's curiosity.

KEY 6: SYNTHESIS—ADDING YOUR OWN THINKING TO WHAT'S IMPORTANT

Synthesizing is closely linked to determining importance. Basically, as we identify what's important, we interweave our thoughts to form a comprehensive perspective to make the whole greater than just the sum of its parts. As Susan and coauthor Ellin Keene put it in their book *Mosaic of Thought:*

> *A mind stretched to a new idea never goes back to its original dimensions.*
>
> —Oliver Wendell Holmes

I remember seeing ancient Byzantine mosaics while traveling in Europe, and being awestruck at the artist's ability to conceptualize a complex and splendid whole while holding only a tiny fragment in his hand. So it is with synthesis.

Synthesis is the process of ordering, recalling, retelling, and recreating into a coherent whole the information with which our minds are bombarded every day. It is the uniquely human trait that permits us to sift through a myriad of details and focus on those pieces we need to know and remember. It is the ability to collect a disparate array of facts and connect them to a central theme or idea. . . . Synthesis is about organizing the different pieces to create a mosaic, a meaning, a beauty, greater than the sum of each shiny piece.

—*MOSAIC OF THOUGHT*, ELLIN OLIVER KEENE AND
SUSAN ZIMMERMANN, PAGE 169

HELPING YOUR CHILD SYNTHESIZE

Start by helping your child retell the most important parts of a story and then pare it down to a simple summary. In fiction, you meet the characters, figure out where and when the story takes place, and are drawn into the plot by dramatic tension: a discovery, an accident, a mystery, a dilemma. This tension keeps you turning pages to find out what happens. A synthesis occurs as you summarize what has happened and what it means to you.

Suppose you've just finished reading *Pink and Say*, Patricia Polacco's poignant Civil War tale. "Here's my summary," you might begin. "This is a powerful story about two young Union soldiers. Pink, a former slave, stumbles upon Say, a wounded white boy lying in a field somewhere in Georgia. Pink saves Say's life by carrying him home to be nursed back to health by his mother, Moe Moe Bay. As Say recovers, the two boys become friends as they learn about each other, dodge marauders, and mourn when the marauders kill Pink's kindhearted mom. They are later captured and sent to the Confederate's dreaded Andersonville prison. Pink is hanged hours after arriving. Say goes on to become a great-grandfather. He is a distant ancestor of Patricia Polacco."

Your child might want to know more about why it was important for both boys to have "touched the hand that touched the hand" of Abraham Lincoln. You might tell about the Emancipation Proclamation and the critical role Lincoln played in freeing the slaves. She might say, "So that's why Pink's mom thought it was such a big deal to touch Say's hand. Lincoln was a hero to them. Now I get it."

You might talk about how Pink felt about slavery:

> To be born a slave is a heap o'trouble, Say. But after Aylee taught me to read, even though he owned my person, I know that nobody, ever, could really own me.
>
> —*PINK AND SAY*, PATRICIA POLACCO, PAGE 21

Those words could spark a conversation about how reading empowered Pink and why returning to the war was more important to him than it was to Say, a 15-year-old from Ohio. You might talk about slavery, discrimination, bravery, and friendship, and about why Polacco wrote the book:

> This book serves as a written memory of Pinkus Aylee since there are no living descendants to do this for him.
>
> When you read this, before you put this book down, say his name out loud and vow to remember him always.
>
> —*PINK AND SAY*, PAGE 44

You and your child will create your own synthesis as you think back over the story: Two boys of different races and backgrounds bound by circumstance share tragedy and hardship, grow to be friends, are separated by death and injustice, and are resurrected through Polacco's story.

When readers synthesize, they identify the essential story line and ask, What does it all mean to me? Readers coax more meaning from the text as they generate questions, apply background knowledge, and discuss it with others. Through the process of synthesizing, their thinking deepens and their understanding grows.

What Kids Say

Determining Importance

- "Do you always try to remember *everything* on the page and then fail a test? Well, then you should try to remember what is important in the text. I would first try to look for text features like bold print or italics. They usually mean that the text you are reading is *extremely* important. Then I would read it again and stop at every paragraph and think, 'Did anything in what I just read contribute to the main idea of the text?' Always ask questions to get more out of the text and to keep your mind on what you are reading. Rereading always gives you a second chance to pick up information on the subject matter. Determining importance is a key skill in reading nonfiction writing."

- "If you've noticed your reading grade plummeting faster than an elephant off a skyscraper, then perhaps it's time for you to read this. The most likely reason for not understanding a book is the lack of concentration. Determining importance is a way to understand what you are reading. It works by separating the facts from everything else. When you understand the facts, you should be able to understand your reading."

- "Determining importance is like a strainer, and the words like noodles in a pot. It sifts out the water and leaves the noodles. In nonfiction, it can be very helpful to leave tracks in the snow (writing around the edges), highlighting and picking *wow* facts [things that you think are more important than the others]. When I look back to before I used determining importance, I can't see how I got by. It's like the light at the end of a tunnel."

—From Debbie Behnfield's fifth-grade class

(continues)

Synthesizing

- "As you collect information from your book, you need to notice your changing thoughts."

- "Synthesizing helps you pick out big details and respond to the story."

- "Synthesizing helps you create a brand-new world in your mind."

- "It's your thinking and background knowledge added to the summary. It helps you understand more about the book."

—FROM MARGARET WING'S THIRD-GRADE CLASS

TIPS FOR PARENTS: DETERMINING IMPORTANCE AND SYNTHESIZING

For Preschool Readers

Your preschool child is learning what's important about life: to look both ways before crossing the street, to share toys with her siblings, to eat healthy food like apples. As you spend time together, talk about what the word "important" means and ask him to share important information with you: "I cut my finger." "I can't find my blankie." "I need to go potty."

The important thing about an apple is that it is round. It is red. You bite it and it is white inside, and the juice splashes in your face, and it tastes like an apple, and it falls off a tree. But the important thing about an apple is that it is round.

—The Important Book,
Margaret Wise Brown

Model what's important to remember in the books you read together. Make this a playful exchange. It won't be long before he'll be offering his choices as well. For young children, often it is the funniest, the spookiest, or the part that reminds them of their own lives that they view as important. That's exactly how it

Books for Determining Importance and Synthesizing

Picture Books

Koala Lou, Mem Fox

Red Leaf, Yellow Leaf, Lois Ehlert

Wild Horse Winter, Tetsuya Honda

Monarch Butterfly, Gail Gibbons

Three Brave Women, C. L. G. Martin

El Chino, Allen Say

And So They Build, Bert Kitchen

Encounter, Jane Yolen

Passage to Freedom, Ken Mochizuki

Rachel's Journal, Marissa Moss

Longer Books

Sarah, Plain and Tall, Patricia MacLachlan (58 pages)

Missing May, Cynthia Rylant (89 pages)

Lewis and Clark: Explorers of the American West,
    Steven Kroll (32 pages)

Sadako and the Thousand Paper Cranes, Eleanor Coerr (79 pages)

Dear Mr. Henshaw, Beverly Cleary (134 pages)

A Boy at War: A Novel of Pearl Harbor, Harry Mazer (104 pages)

Matilda, Roald Dahl (240 pages)

My Louisiana Sky, Kimberly Willis Holt (200 pages)

Hatchet, Gary Paulsen (195 pages)

Tuck Everlasting, Natalie Babbitt (139 pages)

should be. They're learning to be active listeners who can pull out information to better understand what is read.

For example, when you read Gary Paulsen's *The Tortilla Factory*, you could say, "Okay, the golden corn is ground into flour and then kneaded with water to make tortillas. Do you think that's important?"

Your child might reply, "I think it's important that they push and squeeze the dough to make it flat. But the best part is where they *eat* the tortillas with juicy beans!"

For Emerging Readers

Imagine going to a football game and not reacting to the field goals, completed passes, and touchdowns by your team.

Spectators don't sit neutrally in the stands, unmoved by the action. They clap, they cheer, they stand. They are completely engaged.

It's the same with reading. An engaged reader is personally involved. She is thinking, reacting, visualizing, laughing, connecting, responding. She is finding new facts and gaining knowledge. Show your emerging reader that reading is an action sport and that she is the key player.

In response to the cover of *Fireflies in the Night*, by Judy Hawes, you might say, "Looks like we're going to learn a lot about fireflies. I used to catch them on hot summer nights with my sisters in Nebraska. It was such fun. But I always wondered how fireflies make their light. What do you want to know about fireflies?"

> As you read, stop now and then to consider what it's important to remember. Distinguish between facts that are interesting and those that are important.

As you read, stop now and then to consider what's important to remember. Distinguish between facts that are interesting and those that are important. You might say, "I think this information about fireflies spending the first 2 years of their life as beetles before they grow wings is interesting, but not as important to me as this. Look! Putting a jar of fireflies in warm water makes the shine brighter. It says here, 'If you dip the jar in cold water, the firefly lights will fade.' What does that mean to you?"

Your child might say, "The sentence 'These homemade flashlights help them find their way along the dark jungle paths' helps me understand this page about how people in hot countries use the fireflies as flashlights."

She might continue, "So now I'm thinking that it makes sense to use fireflies for light in *hot* places like the jungle, because their shine is brighter. I still don't get how they make that light or why it fades in the cold."

By making decisions about what is important, your child's awareness is heightened. She continues searching for answers about how the insect makes light. The information about using fireflies to light Japanese gardens is interesting, but it's not as important as the fact that "fireflies have special chemicals inside them. When fireflies take in air, the air mixes with these chemicals. Flash!—the mixture makes light without heat."

You might say, "So it's the *air* that sets off the chemicals on the underside of the firefly."

When you show your child how to sift and sort through information, then note how thinking changes as you digest new facts, she'll learn how to deepen her own comprehension.

For Advancing Readers

Your child has just finished reading a couple of books about the Lewis and Clark expedition. He has a report to write, but he's feeling information overload. He needs help determining what's important.

You might say, "Let's try to simplify. If you think back over all you read, what are four things about Lewis and Clark's trip you think are most important? Let's skim the tables of contents and look at the pictures. That'll give a good overview. You can mark with a sticky note the places you think are most important. You might need to lump incidents together to select just four key concepts."

After looking at both books for a while and thinking together, your child might say, "Both books talked about how the 40 men gathered supplies and trained for the long trip. I guess I could mark this first part about what they did to get ready. Then there were all the hard things that happened to them like snowstorms, terrible mosquitoes, crossing the mountains, Indian attacks, getting sick and lost."

"Will you mark all of these things, or do you want to focus on a few of the hardships?"

"I don't know," your child answers.

You might say, "For now, why don't you keep them all in one category. You can think of them as roadblocks to the way west."

Your child says, "I think it was pretty amazing that no white men had ever seen prairie dogs or grizzly bears. Lewis and Clark drew pictures of new plants and animals they saw along the way and sent them to President Jefferson. I think I'll mark these words with sticky notes."

> Lewis and Clark saw buffalo, pelicans, and coyotes, all of which were new to them.... Jefferson had sent the explorers west partly to record the natural world there. Since the camera had not been invented yet, Lewis and Clark had to use paper and pencil to describe and show what they saw.
>
> —*LEWIS AND CLARK*, ANDREW SANTELLA, PAGE 23

Together, you review the various categories of important information concerning Lewis and Clark's expedition, saying, "Okay, so you have 'preparation,' 'roadblocks,' 'recording the natural world.' Those are three good areas. You have one more sticky note. Was there something else mentioned in both sources you think might be important?"

Your child answers, "Both books talked a lot about Sacagawea. I don't think Lewis and Clark would have made it without her."

"What did she do?"

"She was an Indian guide and got them over the mountain passes. She had been stolen from her tribe when she was 13. After she joined up with Lewis and Clark, she stumbled upon her old village. Her brother turned out to be the chief! He gave the men horses and directions to get over the mountain pass. Sacagawea made the whole trip to the Pacific Ocean. Now there's a statue in her honor and her picture is on the dollar coin."

"Do you feel like she should be the fourth thing to focus on?"

"Yeah, I really have a lot to say about Sacagawea."

Through conversations like this, your son will learn how to summarize and organize what he has read to make it manageable and to capture its meaning. You've helped him sift through the facts and identify what's most important.

CLASSROOM CONNECTIONS: DETERMINING IMPORTANCE AND SYNTHESIZING

When teachers model the mental effort involved in determining importance and then provide provocative materials for students to practice on, a shift occurs in the classroom: The search is on to find out what really matters in reading. There's something at stake, and, as a result, students are more engaged.

Crafting Session

The following crafting session and conference took place as Chryse modeled a lesson on determining importance in text.

Deb Behnfield's fifth graders were working on how to determine importance in text. They were learning how to use this strategy to get the essence of what *they* read and to write their science projects in a way that would help others learn new information. Deb and I wanted to see if her students could separate the main ideas from the details of an article and then determine the significance of what's highlighted. To show them how to pull out important information, I shared "Munch a Bunch of Caterpillars," an article from *World* magazine. The students watched me think through the

> *All words are pegs to hang ideas on.*
>
> —Henry Ward Beecher

Crafting Session Tips

- Determining importance has to do with knowing why you're reading and then making decisions about what information or ideas are most critical to understanding the overall meaning of the piece.

- Knowing your purpose for reading is a big factor in determining what's important when you read. It affects how carefully you read and has an impact on what you determine to be important.

- Noting text features helps you lift important information from the text. Often the format of nonfiction text—for example, boxing information, boldfacing ideas, labeling pictures—alerts you to importance.

- To determine importance, you consciously prioritize information to make decisions about what's essential and what is less essential.

- Reading to add to background knowledge directs your search for important information.

- Launching a search to determine important information often starts with the generation of a question.

- Authors leave clues as to what they think is important to remember. Phrases like "as a result" and "in summary" alert you to watch for essential information.

- Summarize important information and then add your thinking as you synthesize to formulate new meaning.

- Synthesize as you use the 7 Keys. Take in the essential facts and ask, What does it all mean to me?

short article, which I showed them on an overhead projector. Whenever a concept was highlighted, I wrote in the margins why I thought it was important. Then, using a format developed by fifth-grade teacher Leslie Blauman, I transferred what I had sorted through to a large poster with three columns headed by the words Main ideas, Details, and Response: lingering thoughts, questions, and connections.

The students watched as I chose one point over another, deciding which of the first two columns to place it in. They talked about why the information went in the Main Ideas or Details column and noted that this process is really a series of judgment calls. Often there is a fine line between the most important idea and supporting details. Sifting through the information itself, not searching for a right or wrong answer, brings a deeper understanding.

When the first two columns were complete, the kids watched me summarize the main concepts, then helped write a response in the third column, where they reacted to the idea of eating caterpillars as a daily supply of minerals and iron.

It was then their turn to determine importance on their own. I summarized three news articles, asked the students to choose which interested them the most, and handed out the three-column response sheet. In the article they selected, they were to practice what I'd just modeled. During independent reading time, I pulled my chair next to Erin's for a conference. She'd chosen an article from the *New York Times*, "Researchers Listen for Whale Clues."

I asked, "Why did you choose this article?"

"I love whales and wanted to read about them. The space junk article didn't seem as interesting, and neither did the one about the turtles in Mexico," Erin said.

"How is this notion of separating three or four important concepts from the less essential details working for you?" I asked. "Looks like you've left some of your thinking in the margins and you've begun to record the main facts on your sheet."

"Well, it really helped to jot down my thinking as I went. Like right here I wrote, 'That's big,' when I read, 'Scientists in the United States and Canada are testing underwater listening devices to pick up the sounds the whales make.' And here I jotted down, 'So that's why they were hunted so much!'"

"Tell me about your thinking when you wrote that in the margins."

"I learned that right whales are easy to hunt because they live close to shore, and this same trait lets them be run over by ships. They just don't get out of the way like other whales do," Erin explained. "I also circled this word and wrote, 'What are buoys?' Reading on, I'm guessing they are things that report back the sound waves." (She needed additional information about buoys to clear up her misunderstanding, and I shared this with her.)

By now the three other students at her table were listening to the conference. Our conversation would help them further their work in their own articles.

From her notes in the margins, Erin had pulled three big concepts from the article, then wrote a more narrative summary of the details:

> When they migrate, they go right through the paths of some major waterways and get killed by ships. Helicopters try to spot them and so do buoys floating in bays. Right whales were named right whales because hunters thought they were right to hunt. They lived close to the shore.

I asked another student at Erin's table to share his main ideas and discuss the thinking behind his decision making. Erin ended up moving the concepts about the role of the buoys and the helicopters trying to spot the whales to the MAIN IDEAS column.

After highlighting her article for importance, organizing her thinking on the three-column sheet, and discussing her ideas, Erin wrote:

> I have heard of right whales before and how they are endangered. They were really vulnerable to hunters. . . . They were just the "right" kind and that's how they got their name. That's cool how they

can track whales just from listening to them. I wonder how they can contact boats in time to help them avoid hitting a whale. If a ship didn't see the whale, the ship might not get a message until it had already run it over. Listening for whales sounds like a plan that would actually work, much more than trying to spot them from the air and the ship.

Erin's understanding was deepened through the process of identifying what was most important to her, talking about the article, bringing up her questions and background knowledge, and developing a synthesis of the piece.

Questions to Reveal Thinking

The following are questions to help students investigate determining importance in text and synthesizing, once you've modeled the concept in crafting sessions:

- What was your purpose for reading this piece? How did your purpose help you figure out what was most important? Could you share how this worked for you with the rest of the class?

- How is coding the text working for you? Oh, you marked two places where you learned something new. Good for you! So being aware of adding on to your background knowledge helps you pull out information that's new and important to you. How does this help you make sense of what you just read?

- Look back over this part. What has the author done to signal what is important to remember? Great—you're using the picture and caption to help you determine what is most important. What other text feature helps lift important information off this page? Yes, these words are in italics. They really do stand up off the page! Let's add this discovery to our chart about how to determine importance.

- I notice you've jotted down two questions about this piece. I can see this first question came from the title. I wonder about that too! Now, how are these questions helping you read for important information? Great! You've found the answer to the first question in this paragraph. Is this second question something you still want to figure out? Yes! Then you plan to keep reading with this question in mind. How does generating questions help you sort through all this information to pull out what is important?

- As you read that passage, what was most important here, what is essential to remember? Yes, this passage is full of information! This part right here is really interesting. When you compare these two parts, which holds more importance for the whole piece? How did you decide?

- We've been talking about how to use key words to help us more efficiently find the information we need, without having to read the whole book. How is this working for you? Show me how you started to find information on _____ . Great—you used the index, went to the page, and skimmed over these paragraphs to find the key phrases you were looking for. Now, how will you capture this information in your report?

- Today I modeled how to reread the clues I uncovered in a book I read yesterday. Then, after putting all the clues together, I tried to come up with the overall big message in the story. I notice you've marked several clues in your book with sticky notes. Let's review what you've figured out. Your marked passages are like a road map. The clues point you to something important. The author hasn't told you to notice these parts but has written in a way for you to make a discovery on your own. What's your thinking now as to the message in this story? Yes, it is hard to put this together on your own! You've made a great start here with these two clues. I'm going to leave you now to keep doing this great detective work. I'll check back with you tomorrow to see how it's going.

- Do you think this author was for or against this idea? How can you tell? What information did he present to build evidence for his case? Here's a highlighter to help you figure out what the author thinks is important to remember. He's used some signal words to make his point. I'm eager to hear what you figure out.

- You've just done a great summary about the information you've learned about Mars. What does it all mean to you? Oh, you just raised a question. How will having that question help you to continue on with your inquiry report? Going to another source to see if it's answered is a smart plan.

- Has your thinking changed after reading this passage? As you read through this article, show me where you noticed your ideas changing. You know, when we synthesize to re-member what we read, we sometimes find we missed impor-tant information that was shared. What is the reader's job when this happens? Yes, rereading to clarify what we missed is a great idea.

- What advice would you give readers outside our class on how to determine important information in nonfiction writing? What advice would you give to those who want to figure out the big message in fiction writing? How does sifting out im-portant facts and ideas, and then adding our thinking back, help you as a reader?

Teachers and Parents Together

- Interview parents about how to determine importance outside of school. How do parents make decisions about which dish-washer to buy; what's the most important attraction to visit in Cody, Wyoming; when to buy and sell stocks; how to recycle old computers; how to vote on the ballot amendments; which vitamins to take; what's the best insulation for the attic.

- Bring the world of nonfiction into the classroom. Parents can help supply travel brochures, catalogues, maps, restaurant guides, how-to manuals, charts, pamphlets, field guides, magazines, and newspapers. Children can investigate how information is organized and highlighted. Noting layout and text features will help students learn to relay their own information in written reports, posters, and science displays.

- Parents have firsthand knowledge on a range of topics from Martin Luther King Jr. to scaling the Andes. As parents are interviewed, students learn how to take notes on what's important and then personalize their learning by synthesizing what was shared.

CHAPTER 7

Cultivating Awareness

KEY 7: FIX-UP STRATEGIES

It is the reader who must attribute meaning to a system of signs, and then decipher it. We all read ourselves and the world around us in order to glimpse what and where we are. We read to understand, or to begin to understand. We cannot do but read. Reading, almost as much as breathing, is our essential function.

—ALBERTO MANGUEL

THIS CHAPTER FOCUSES on strategies for readers to use when they are stumped and need help to get back on the comprehension track.

💡 Enlighten Yourself First

September 22, 2002. Paul and I are hiking in southeast Utah's Canyonlands. Torrential rains had poured for 2 days before we arrived. The skies have cleared, leaving a chill in the air and a surprising amount of water. In places that are usually bone dry, clear pools have formed in pockets in the stone. Today we are backpacking out of Chesler Park, an immense upland meadow surrounded by huge gnomelike rock formations striped pink and cream. Our destination is Lost Canyon. We're up, ready to go, and pause just long enough to watch the full moon setting over the contorted red rock of the Maze District. Although we are avid hikers, this is new to us. We've never hiked in terrain this dry and rugged.

The map shows a 6-mile hike to our next camp. Piece of cake, I think, knowing my pack is significantly lighter than it was 3 days ago when we hiked into Chesler. We follow a steep pitch down into Elephant Canyon, hook onto a trail along the canyon bottom for a mile, then turn sharply and begin climbing the pass between Elephant and Big Spring Canyons. As we ascend, we leave the footpath behind and climb a slickrock pass with only cairns, strategically placed piles of rocks, to guide us. At an impasse, we come to a 15-foot wooden ladder, climb it, traverse a narrow causeway, and climb down a metal ladder on the other side. We stay high above the canyons, walking on red and gray slickrock, looking out to a surreal landscape of rock spires and stone profiles, hobgoblins and royalty carved by wind and water. It is a long drop to the canyon floor. We follow the cairns, our lifeline to civilization in this wild, remote country.

We hike, chat, admire the view, drink from our Camelbacks, and realize all of a sudden that our conscientious effort to follow the cairns has failed. There isn't one in sight. We spend a few minutes searching for a cairn in the near vicinity. No luck. Paul sheds his pack and scouts ahead, returning to report that the way forward is impassable. Pulling out the map, we chart our progress, but remain baffled, unable to pinpoint exactly where we are or discover a way to Big Spring Canyon. Paul gets out the compass and orients it on the map. Still, we're stumped.

Finally, backtracking, we find the last cairn we passed. Glancing up, Paul spots a cairn on a rock ledge overhead and says, "Look, we must have to go up over this." My heart sinks. Paul scrambles up. We tie in his pack and hoist it up to the ledge. I'm pretty sure no amount of hoist will get me to where he is.

All of a sudden, he shouts, "Where the heck did you come from?"

Out of nowhere comes a woman's voice. "From Big Spring Canyon," she says.

"How?" asked Paul.

"Through the crack up near those trees."

I walk to where I catch sight of a strong woman, clearly at ease in the desert, walking up a steep pitch of slickrock. "You're our guardian angel!" I yell.

"Glad I could help."

Paul descends from the ledge. We hike up to the cluster of trees and see what looks like a dark, narrow cave behind it. Upon closer inspection, we detect a cairn, a log with foot notches carved out, and a narrow crack that shows light on the other side. We scramble through a 200-foot-long joint in the rock and make it through to Big Spring Canyon. Back on track, we carry forward to our destination.

—SUSAN

Call them fix-up strategies, backup plans, safety nets. Whatever they are called, it's necessary to know how to use them for many things in life. It's also necessary to know *when* they are needed or else they are no help.

A lot of kids don't realize they've lost their way when they read. They think if they rush through the words and turn the pages, they're "getting through it." They are, but they're not getting anything *out* of it. They need fix-up strategies. The best fix-up strategy of all is to cultivate awareness: to be so engaged with the text that when that engagement starts to waver, just like a car veering from its lane, they immediately recognize it and can take steps to get back on course.

WHAT IS "FIXING UP"?

The 7 Keys themselves are overarching fix-ups. They help turn kids into engaged readers. Kids become more aware of their thinking when they read with the keys in mind.

> A lot of kids don't realize they've lost their way when they read. They think if they rush through the words and turn the pages, they're "getting through it."

If the motion picture in a reader's minds shuts down, he knows he needs to slow down, reread, and get the movie back rolling in his head. If no questions arise, he knows he needs to stop daydreaming and focus. If nothing seems important in what he reads, he knows he needs to figure out why. If he's making no connections between the text and his life or the larger world, he needs to stop, take stock, and think more deliberately of what background knowledge he has and what he needs to build. If he can't retell, or put what he's read into his own words, it's a signal he's not understanding. Learning how to use the 7 Keys is a major step toward becoming a reader with a toolbox full of effective fix-ups.

But sometimes the 7 Keys are not enough. Readers need more: a compass, a map, an expert, and a little backtracking.

A few years ago on a raft trip on the San Juan River, Susan's family came to a fork at an island. Without much thought, they headed river right. Several hundred yards farther, their boat got hung up in a long stretch of shallow, cobble-filled water. At the end of an achingly exhausting day, they had to pull their heavily loaded boat upstream against a rushing current until they were back at the fork, able to board again and float on without a struggle.

"We must've learned something from that," Susan moaned, "but I can't imagine what."

Her daughter Helen quipped, "Hey, Mom. Sometimes you have to go backward to go forward."

It's exactly the same with reading. Sometimes you find yourself in unfamiliar terrain. You've never read a book that has such challenging vocabulary. You've never read about fly-fishing, or Egyptian history, or genetics. It's tough going, and you need strategies to make your way through it safely and meaningfully. Rereading ("going backward to go forward") is one of the best fix-up strategies there is. Often, a simple reread—this time with more concentration—will get a child back on track if he has lost his train of thought or encountered a challenging word.

The book *Pinkish, Purplish, Bluish Egg* begins:

Myrtle was sad and completely depressed
As she sat staring down at her empty dove's nest;
Her children had flown off and left her that day . . .

—*Pinkish, Purplish, Bluish Egg*, Bill Peet, page 1

The word *depressed* might stump your child first time through. If she reads this passage a couple of times, she'll probably figure it out because any mother would be heartsick if her children had grown up and left her.

But merely rereading might leave your child frustrated and just as clueless as he was the first time through. The reread has to include some conscious problem solving. He has to identify the problem. He has to consciously pull out his fix-up tools and use them. Are there difficult words that need to be figured out? Does the piece have confusing grammar? Does he need to know more about a certain topic to "get it"? Would it help if he talked to a friend about it, or does he need to go to someone who is an expert? The expert can be a parent, friend, teacher, someone who knows the subject matter, an encyclopedia, or a dictionary.

WHAT DOES NOT UNDERSTANDING LOOK LIKE?

Our good friend Cris Tovani works with high school students who are struggling readers. She's a masterful teacher who has turned on many students to reading when everyone else has given up on them. She focuses on finding their passions, respecting their opinions, and teaching them the thinking strategies so they know *how* to engage in what they read. She also lets the students know that it is *their* job to comprehend, not hers. No one can do the comprehending for anyone else, so the reader has to know when he's not getting it.

We've adapted the following six signals for alerting readers when they are stuck from Cris's book, *I Read It, But I Don't Get It*:

1. The voice in my head changes. I stop having a conversation with the text and just cover the words. Quickly, I'm either bored or confused and probably won't remember what I've read.

2. The camera inside my head shuts off. I no longer have a mental picture of what I'm reading. This is a good indication that understanding has been interrupted.

3. My mind starts to wander and I'm thinking about all sorts of different things, but not about what I'm reading. I know then I need to reconnect.

4. I can't remember what I just read. I should be able to retell what I read. If not, I know I need to go back, concentrate, and focus more on understanding.

5. I'm not asking or answering questions as I go. When questions don't get asked or answered, I probably need more background knowledge or I need to focus more purposefully on the text.

6. I encounter characters and have no memory of when they were introduced. I haven't kept track of what's happening.

Once your child realizes she is confused or has zoned out, she *can* do something about it. Here are some fix-up tools to use if she's not understanding:

- Go back and reread. Sometimes that is enough.

- Read ahead to clarify meaning.

- Identify what it is you don't understand: word, sentence, or concept.

- If it is a word, read beyond it and see if its meaning is clarified later in the text, or think about the content so far and predict what word might make sense. If those approaches don't work, ask someone what it means or look it up in a dictionary.

- If it is a sentence in a picture book, look at the pictures and think about what has happened so far; then reread, and read ahead, to see if understanding comes. If you're still confused, talk with a friend, parent, or teacher about it.

- If it is a concept, try to summarize the story up to the confusing spot. See if that clears up the confusion. It might be necessary to build more background knowledge. That means going to an encyclopedia, checking out the Internet, having a conversation with someone who knows about the topic, or doing research at the library.

PEANUTS REPRINTED BY PERMISSION OF UNITED FEATURE SYNDICATE, INC.

Examples of Fix-Ups

Susan's son Mark is, like many 16-year-old boys, a would-be rock star. Recently, he made the plunge from an acoustic to an electric guitar. At the Guitar Center checkout, where Susan purchased the guitar, this note was posted:

> Due to a typographical error, the Epiphone Les Paul Junior shown on p. 26 of our 38th anniversary guide states that it has a P-90 pickup. That statement and the picture shown are incorrect. The pickup is actually a humbucker.
>
> We apologize for any inconvenience this may have caused.

Susan could not possibly have been inconvenienced, because she had absolutely no idea what they were talking about. She could figure out that the Epiphone Les Paul Junior was a type of guitar. She understood that an error had been made in their catalogue, but she had no idea what a humbucker was. Until she knew the meaning of that word, she couldn't make sense of their apology. To "fix up" this failure to comprehend, she had to find an expert in electric guitars. He was standing behind the counter and informed her, "Yeah, we've had customers who were real upset about this. Basically, a normal pickup on an electric guitar allows a buzz. A humbucker is two of the normal pickups coiled together tightly to prevent the buzz. It bucks the hum." Mystery solved.

Let's say your advanced reader encounters a passage such as the following:

> In no position to resist the English incursion, the local Wampanoag Indians at first befriended the settlers. Cultural accommodation was facilitated by Squanto, a Wampanoag who had learned English from a ship's captain who had kidnapped him some years earlier. . . . As more English settlers arrived and pushed inland into the Connecticut River valley, confrontations between Indians and whites ruptured these peaceful relations. . . . Besieging a Pequot village on Connecti-

cut's Mystic River, English militia men and their Narrangansett Indian allies set fire to the Indian wigwams and shot the fleeing survivors. The slaughter wrote a brutal finish to the Pequot War.

—*THE AMERICAN PAGEANT*, THOMAS A. BAILEY AND
DAVID M. KENNEDY, PAGE 50

Your child might be able to pronounce all these words but not grasp the meaning. Being a mindful reader involves not only reciting the words but also understanding what those words mean in context. Is your child aware of what she understands and what she doesn't? Does she need to look up words like "incursion," "Wampanoag," "ruptured"? Does she have adequate background knowledge about this historical reference?

> Being a mindful reader involves not only reciting the words but also understanding what those words mean in context.

The point is she needs to know when there is a breakdown at the word level and when the breakdown is at the concept level. If it is a conceptual breakdown, chances are good that she'll need to consciously build her background knowledge through conversations in class and additional study. For a word breakdown, she might be able to infer the meaning by rereading. If that doesn't work, she can check the dictionary or ask a knowledgeable friend. Mainly, it's important that your child realize that when she is off track she can't just read on mindlessly. She needs to stop, take stock of the situation, and figure out what type of fix-up strategy she needs to pull out of her toolbox.

 ## TIPS FOR PARENTS: FOSTERING AWARENESS AND USING FIX-UP STRATEGIES

For Preschool Readers

Young children can follow a story and judge when it makes sense and when it doesn't. Praise your child if he catches you incorrectly para-

What Kids Say

Cultivating Reading Awareness

- "Where am I?" (Lost meaning, so reread)

- "Hmm . . . " (Reacted to the text, then made conscious decision to keep reading)

- "I didn't know that!" (Added new information to background knowledge)

- "You've got to be kidding!" (Stopped to think and then reread)

- "Say what?" (Stopped to think and then posed a question)

- "Been there before." (Text-to-self connection)

- "Huh?" (Reread to clarify)

- "Yes!" (Hardy agreement with the author)

- "Who is talking here?" (Self-questioned, reread, summarized)

- "Just like that other book." (Text-to-text connection)

- "This is huge." (Determined importance)

- "Love these words!" (Enjoyed!)

- "I bet that . . ." (Drew an inference)

- "Where are they?" (Tried to visualize)

- "Now I think . . ." (Synthesized new thoughts)

- "No clue." (Monitored a breakdown; consulted a friend about concept)

—FROM PAULA BOWERS'S FIFTH-GRADE CLASS

phrasing the last few pages of a favorite bedtime story. He's building his listening skills, and your rendition didn't quite add up. Congratulate him when he notices a skipped page. He's keeping a record of the story line and detects that it has suddenly been interrupted.

Make a game of "getting it": Pause and summarize the story line thus far. If you get lost, share your confusion, and model what you do to get back on track. Say you're reading Ian Falconer's *Olivia Saves the Circus*. It's easy to follow the actions of confident Olivia as she makes breakfast for her brothers and accessorizes her boring school uniform with red bows and striped tights.

You might say, "I get these pages. Olivia's starting the day, eating pancakes, picking out her clothes, and flying off to school on her scooter. Can't you just see that red backpack bumping up and down as she pushes along? Then she stands up in front of the class and tells them all about her vacation. That's when I get a little confused. Listen: 'One day my mother took Ian and me to the circus,' she begins. 'William couldn't come because he still has to nap. But when we got there, all the circus people were out sick with ear infections.'"

You give your child a quizzical look. "How can they have a circus without performers? Let's keep reading to find out."

You've just shared a critical fix-up option: making a conscious decision to read on to clarify meaning. You "get it" when Olivia's imagination kicks in and she steps right up to tame the lions and walk the tightrope.

What It Means to Be an Active Reader

Listen to the voice in your head that always bugs you and use it. . . . If there are questions, answer them. Keep your mental picture in your head, and let that little voice work. Do I understand? Do I not get it? Write questions, comments, "I wonder," and even lingering thoughts. Determining importance happens when you find something important: Highlight it, ask questions about it, and connect with it. If any of these pieces of advice help you, don't thank me—thank that annoying voice in your head!

—FROM A STUDENT IN DEBBIE BEHNFIELD'S FIFTH-GRADE CLASS

Books That Help Cultivate Awareness

Picture Books

The Paper Bag Princess, Robert Munsch

Chrysanthemum, Kevin Henkes

The Birthday Thing, SuAnn and Kevin Kiser

Thunder Cake, Patricia Polacco

A Day's Work, Eve Bunting

Longer Books

Baseball, Snakes, and Summer Squash: Poems About Growing Up, Donald Graves (80 pages)

Two-Minute Mysteries, Donald J. Sobol (158 pages)

Homeless Bird, Gloria Whelan (186 pages)

Bridge to Terabithia, Katherine Paterson (128 pages)

The Lion, the Witch, and the Wardrobe, C. S. Lewis (206 pages)

Later, when Olivia's teacher questions her and she says it's a true story—"To the best of my recollection"—you might be a little confused: "Wait. I'm not getting this part. What do you think she means when she says it's a true vacation story?"

Your child might reply, "She's *pretending*, Mom. She doesn't *really* walk on stilts or ride a unicycle, but that's the best part. Let's read it again!"

Keep the tone relaxed as you play the "get it" game. Laugh together when you change predictions, recall background knowledge, recap to the confusing spot, reread, and read ahead. You're teaching your child to solve comprehension snags.

For Emerging Readers

Emerging readers can recognize and pronounce a steady stream of words. As they work their way through a story, they might experience breakdowns when faced with unfamiliar vocabulary. Providing tips about how to figure out new words is key for them.

Say you're reading Marissa Moss's *Regina's Big Mistake*. You talk about what Regina's mistake might be, getting clues from the cover and title. You read the first few pages to get the story started: "Everyone was supposed to draw a jungle or a rain forest. That meant Regina, too."

Your child takes over: "She started to draw a jungle flower. She drew one petal, then another."

The word *petal* causes a breakdown as he reads out loud. You could just tell him the word so the sentence flows naturally, but you might decide to demonstrate how readers figure out unfamiliar words so he'll be able to do it on his own later: "This is a tricky word. Let's look at the picture, then read the sentence again and say 'hmm' when we come to this word. Maybe we can figure it out. 'She drew one *hmm*, then another.' What word would make sense here?"

This could be just enough of a hint for him figure out the word is *petal*. But what if he still has no clue?

You might say, "Let's think about what's happened so far in the story. We know Regina is having trouble drawing anything. On this page, it looks like she's beginning to put some lines on the paper. She's drawing a flower. When I think about flowers, it helps me predict that this word could be 'petal.' Do you think 'petal' sounds right, looks right, and makes sense?"

You've shown your child a fix-up process to help him figure out new words on his own.

For Advancing Readers

Sharon Creech's *Walk Two Moons* is a heartwarming tale that calls on all of the thinking strategies. From one chapter to the next, you'll raise questions, describe the scenes in your mind, offer predictions, note what's important, recall what's happened, and realize when it's not making sense. Let's look at this short passage, narrated by 13-year-old Sal.

> On the night that we got the bad news—that she (Sal's mother) was not returning—he pounded and pounded on that wall with a chisel and a hammer. At two o'clock in the morning, he came up to my room. I was not asleep. He led me downstairs and showed me what he had found. Hidden behind the wall was a brick fireplace.
>
> The reason that Phoebe's story reminds me of that plaster wall and the hidden fireplace is that beneath Phoebe's story was another one. Mine.
>
> —*WALK TWO MOONS*, SHARON CREECH, PAGE 3

You might say, "This is confusing. I wonder why Sal's mother isn't coming back. Her dad must be pretty upset to be tearing up the house like that. I'm wondering if he's sad or angry. I'm also wondering what Phoebe's story is all about. I don't get how Sal's story is hidden beneath hers." These questions alert you to important details ahead. Sharing them heightens your curiosity to get on with the story.

To escape the past, Sal and her dad move from the family home in Kentucky, but their sad memories follow them to Euclid, Ohio, where the story unfolds. Mysterious messages begin to appear. There's a potential lunatic on the loose. Scenes of Sal's new life roll through your mind as you picture her new home jammed between other houses "like a row of birdhouses."

With questions to be answered and mental images playing, you and your child can periodically recap what's happened to strengthen your understanding and speculate about what's to come.

Suppose you had to put down *Walk Two Moons*. You might pick it up several weeks later and need a refresher to pick up where you left off. Show your child how good readers do a quick summary to get back on track: "Remember, there are two tales going on in this book.

Sal is telling her grandparents the story of how Phoebe's mom disappeared. At the same time, we're in on the adventures she's having with her grandparents as they ride across the country to find Sal's own mom. Also, notes keep appearing on Phoebe's doorstep, but I can't remember what that last one said. Let's find it."

You reread this passage:

> As I walked home, I thought about the message. *In the course of a lifetime, what does it matter?* I said it over and over. I wondered about the mysterious messenger, and I wondered about all the things in the course of a lifetime that would not matter. I did not think cheerleading tryouts would matter, but I was not so sure about yelling at your mother. I was certain, however, that if your mother left, it would be something that mattered in the whole long course of your lifetime.
>
> —*WALK TWO MOONS*, PAGE 106

Thinking back to the story, your child might say, "Phoebe is afraid of everything, but Sal is the one who really has problems. That's what really matters."

Together you and your child summarize the book up to where you stopped and refresh your memory by rereading the last passage. Now you're back on track, ready to work your way to the book's ending.

 ## CLASSROOM CONNECTIONS: MONITORING FOR MEANING

Thinking about reading involves being aware of what your mind does as you create meaning. It's about turning on the thought process *before* you read and paying attention *while* you read. It's about playing an active role in tracking understanding and knowing how to fix comprehension when you get lost. When students learn how to do this for themselves, they read it and get it on their own.

> *What is reading but silent conversation?*
> —Walter Savage Landor

Crafting Session

Teachers can evaluate reading progress as students successfully decode sounds, words, and sentences. To assess mastery of the text, the teacher listens to students read aloud, asks for retellings about what was read, and keeps records of their progress. But students also need to *think* about their reading. Monitoring when they get it and knowing when they don't are critical. Chryse worked with a group of first graders to help them monitor their reading.

Working with one group of first graders, I noticed that although they were building their reading speed, few were giving themselves thinking time. In their effort to read quickly, they missed important information. I needed to slow them down and show them that flying through the words wasn't enough. They needed to understand.

On the wall, I taped a large piece of butcher paper divided into three headings: REREAD, STOP AND THINK, READ ON. The kids gathered for the crafting session. I chose a "secretary" from the group to chart my thinking and handed him a marker to keep track.

"You're all doing well using background knowledge to better understand what you read," I began. "Today I'd like to share something else readers do to make sense of words. Good readers 'turn on' their thinking as they read. They notice when they understand what they are reading and when they are stuck. Then great readers take action to get unstuck!

"Let me show you how this works. My secretary is going to keep track of my thinking on the chart. He'll mark each time he catches me rereading, stopping to think, and reading on. Don't worry if he misses a few. Your job as listeners is to enjoy the story and watch how I not only read the words and the pictures but think about my thinking as I go through the story.

"Hmm, as I read the title—*Gilimoto*—by Karen Lynn Williams, and look at the picture on the cover, I stop and think: Is Gilimoto the name of a town, or the name of the boy who looks like he's building something, or the name of what he's building? I'll just have to read on to find out."

Crafting Session Tips

- When you're engaged with the text, you recognize when meaning wavers.
- It is the reader's job to know when the text makes sense and when it doesn't.
- When readers have trouble visualizing what's going on, are unable to retell what they've read, lack questions or predictions, can't find connecting points, haven't learned anything new, and aren't enjoying what they are reading, it means they need to apply fix-up options.
- Being aware of when you're connecting with what you read is key.
- Good readers stop when there's a comprehension breakdown, take stock of the situation, and figure out how to fix the problem.

Fix-up options include the following:

- Rereading
- Reading ahead
- Raising new questions
- Drawing inferences
- Making predictions
- Figuring out unknown words
- Seeking help from an outside source
- Stopping to think
- Connecting the reading to background knowledge
- Trying to get a mental image
- Looking at sentence structure
- Inspecting pictures and other text features
- Reading the author's note
- Writing about confusing parts
- Consciously thinking about the piece's message
- Defining the purpose for why we're reading in the first place

My secretary made a dramatic check under STOP AND THINK and another under READ ON. As I read and thought out loud through the story, I paused every few pages to model confusion, so REREAD and READ ON got checks, but mostly I paused to think. As I stopped to think, I shared with the kids my questions, connections, and predictions. By the time the story ended, my thinking had been visibly tracked. And STOPPING TO THINK won hands down.

In the following weeks, the children practiced taking stock of their thinking as they paused to note the spots with sticky notes in the books they'd chosen to read. The sticky notes preserved their thinking for later conferences and sharing sessions.

In another crafting session, the kids kept track of their thinking on butcher paper. They sketched and wrote their understandings and confusions as I paused to think aloud. Each day the students added suggestions to the chart labeled "What do you do when you don't understand?" This type of chart showed what we collectively learned about being an active reader.

We used our sharing sessions to talk about what it sounds and looks like in our minds when we get it, and what actions we take when we don't. The kids shared their thinking during conferences with me, and some even bravely did "think-alouds" for the class. By publicly sharing what they did when they hit a snag, they became more aware of the importance of being engaged readers who knew when they didn't understand and had the tools to do something about it.

Questions to Reveal Thinking

Ask the following questions to discover if your students are monitoring for meaning.

- You've come to a word you don't know. What have you tried so far to figure it out? Good for you. You just predicted a word that could work in this sentence.

- At what point did the story stop making sense for you? How did you notice there was a problem in your understanding? What did you do to get back on track?

- You've marked this passage with a sticky note, which shows that you stopped to think about your reading. Please read the words and share what was on your mind. Great—you've thought about your own experience, and that helped you make sense of what you read.

- You read this paragraph perfectly. What do you remember about what you just read? You know, sometimes that happens to me. I say the words in my head but don't have my thinking turned on. What do you need to do now to get the meaning from the words?

- You seem to be confused by this part. It's great that you've noticed you're stuck. Are you having problems understanding some of these words, or are you confused by what's going on?

- Good for you. You just went back to the spot where meaning broke down and reread from that point. What do you understand now that you didn't understand before? What do you think will happen next?

- We've been talking about some fix-up strategies we could use when meaning breaks down. How is this working for you? Oh, you noticed you could visualize what was happening on this page, but you lost the mental image here. I'm glad you're aware when your "reading camera" shuts off. What do you think caused this? You know, I think figuring out this word will help get the camera rolling again.

- Sometimes making a conscious decision to keep reading clears up confusion. Share the question you have right now. Good for you. Having that question in mind as you read on will help you repair the breakdown in understanding.

- How do you know when you understand what you've read? One way we keep track of meaning is to tell ourselves what's happened so far. We pull out the important parts and think about what it all means to us. Would you share with the class how this works for you?

- As you talked about your thinking, you relied on retelling and connecting to uncover the meaning. Good for you! The strategies overlap, and knowing this will help you better understand what you read.

- What advice would you give someone outside our class about how to monitor for meaning and how to fix up confusion?

Teachers and Parents Together

- Have students pick a difficult passage for their parents to figure out. Have parents talk about what they do to get unstuck. Make a list of all the fix-up tools parents use to clear up meaning.

- Create flyers offering advice about what you do when you come to a word you don't know. This would include allowing time to think it through, checking to see if the word makes sense and looks right, sounding it out, and rereading. Creativity welcome!

- Have students survey parents about what they do in their jobs when they don't understand what's going on. What plans do carpenters consult when they hit a snag? How do auto mechanics troubleshoot? What about surgeons? Identify common problem-solving approaches.

CHAPTER 8

Visible and Invisible Reading Ingredients

As [the reader] brings the text to life, he casts back and forth in his head for connections between what he is reading and what he already knows. His eyes scan forward or jump backwards. He pauses, pushes on, selects from his memory whatever relates the meaning to his experience or his earlier reading, in a rich and complex system of to-ing and fro-ing in his head, storing, reworking, understanding, or being puzzled.

—MARGARET MEEK

READING IS LIKE making chocolate chip cookies. You don't need *just* flour or butter or eggs or sugar or vanilla extract or chocolate chips. You need them all, combined together. The flour and butter and eggs provide what we could call *surface structure*. They are essential. You need them to make the cookie. But they're not distinctive, and they're not enough. They could be the start for any old cookie. It's the vanilla and chocolate chips that give the cookie its particular flavor. They provide what we'll call the *deep structure*, the *meaning*.

It's the same with reading. There are surface structure and deep structure ingredients. You need all of them to get to true comprehension.

You can help your child become a great reader without knowing about surface and deep structure systems. But for those parents who are searching for a clearer understanding of all that goes into reading, this chapter will put it into perspective.

For many years the conventional wisdom was that once children could sound out words, they could read. Now experts know it's not that simple. There's a whole lot more to reading. Phonics (sounding out words) is like the flour in the chocolate chip cookie. You can't manage without it, but by itself it accomplishes little.

Too often, children grow up with some of the reading ingredients, but not all. They might stumble over letters or words. They might read so slowly that they can't remember what they read earlier. They might read easily and swiftly, but when you ask them to talk about what they've read, they can't tell you. For these children, a critical part of the reading mix is missing. To read well, all the ingredients are needed.

NECESSARY INGREDIENTS OF THE READING MIX

The surface ingredients comprise the visible side of reading. Children need to know which sounds go with which letters. They need to be able to sight-read whole words without having to sound out each syllable. They also need to understand the architecture of language, how words are strung together to make sense, and how grammar and punctuation organize sentences. In other words, they have to "break the code" at the levels of the letter, the word, and the sentence. Surface structure deals with identifying, recognizing, and pronouncing words and sentences.

But code breaking is not reading. It's decoding. Children need to grasp the *meaning* of words in context. They need to use their background knowledge to better understand what they read. And they need to be able to read differently depending upon their purpose for reading. That's where the deep structure—which deals with the invisible side of reading—comes into play. This invisible side of reading is vital. Without it, the reader doesn't understand. The 7 Keys are closely linked to the deep structure part of reading, because they are the tools necessary for the conscious and thoughtful harvesting of meaning.

The visible and invisible systems provide the six essential ingredients that every child needs to become a good reader. Children do not learn all this in a fixed, sequential manner. They learn the visible and invisible systems simultaneously.

> This invisible side of reading is vital. Without it, the reader doesn't understand.

In fact, as soon as you started talking to your baby, she began the process of learning language. She developed an oral understanding of words, sentences, and stories way before she was able to decode the written word. She could use elaborate sentences, wrap you around her little finger, follow complicated instructions, and understand complex stories long before she could "do phonics" or read on her own. She accomplished this without an hour of classroom time. The point: You are your child's first and most important teacher. The time she spends with you talking, being read to, and playing is fundamental to developing the surface and deep structure systems that she later uses as a reader.

As you read this chapter, don't panic. You don't have to remember all the ingredients or have a Ph.D. in reading to support your child as she becomes a great reader. The point is to give you an overview of what's involved in reading so you have a broader perspective and better understanding of how the ingredients add up to create a good reader. You'll know better what you can do to make the reading journey a joyful one. You'll be better equipped to spot problems if they arise.

Remember, although we are setting these ingredients out in a sequence, *all* of them are vitally important. Your child learns phonics at the same time that she learns the meanings of words and learns the different purposes for reading and pursuing a passionate interest in bugs, airplanes, or outer space. The batter is being mixed well!

Finally, be sure to create a loving, comfortable, and *fun* environment for your child so that she views reading as pleasure, *not* pain. Use the 7 Keys to enhance and develop your child's thinking about what you read to her or what she reads on her own. You're stirring everything together to create a delicious result: a child who loves to read because she reads it and gets it.

VISIBLE INGREDIENTS: SURFACE STRUCTURES

1. Letter/Sound Knowledge (Phonics)

Several years ago, Susan and her husband, Paul, drove through Athens. Map in hand, they were confident they could maneuver through the city. It hadn't occurred to them that a map printed in English would do little good in Greece. The street signs, written with the Greek alphabet, were indecipherable. The traffic whizzed past, and the 4 hours they'd allotted to get to the Athens airport disintegrated in the confusion of making one turn after another with no idea where they were. The phrase "It's Greek to me" took on new meaning. Ultimately, they pulled off the road and flagged down a cab. The driver spoke just enough English to discern they'd pay him *anything* to lead them to the airport.

Adults rarely understand what our children experience when first confronted with written language. If you meet someone who can read Chinese, Japanese, or Arabic, you tend to think he is really smart because he can "break codes" that you can't. It looks impossible. But what he does is no different from what you do and what young children do every day: He deciphers and makes sense of written language. It's just that he has learned a different alphabet or characters.

In Athens, Susan was completely closed out of the language because she had no knowledge of the letter/sound connections. The letters on the Athens street signs were meaningless scratches, because she didn't have the key to unlock the Greek alphabet.

The Reading Ingredients

The following chart is adapted from *Toward an Interactive Model of Reading.*

Visible Ingredients: Surface Structures

1. Letter/sound knowledge (phonics)

    - Recognizing letters

    - Recognizing sounds that go with letters

2. Word knowledge (lexical)

    - Recognizing words without needing to "sound out"

    - Identifying whole words rapidly

3. Structure of language (syntax)

    - Hearing when sentences sound right and when they don't

    - Recognizing correct grammar and punctuation

Invisible Ingredients: Deep Structures

4. Word meanings/associations (semantics)

    - Understanding the meanings of words in different contexts

    - Noting the shades of meaning in words and phrases

5. Background knowledge (schema)

    - Using background knowledge to enhance understanding

    - Knowing whether there is a need to build background knowledge in order to understand

6. Knowledge of audience/purpose (pragmatic)

    - Understanding the purpose for specific reading

    - Reading differently depending upon the purpose.

One of the ways children learn letter/sound connections is by writing. Since she was 4 years old, Chryse's daughter Liz left notes scattered around the house. By looking at picture books, an animal alphabet chart, nursery rhymes, the backs of cereal boxes, she had learned various letter/sound connections and used them to get her point across. Taped to the last piece of pie would be a note warning, "et at yr on rsk." On carefully built block constructions, she'd tape "do nt rek."

Writing messages helped Liz solidify what she'd learned about the sounds letters make. And, as her family responded to her instructions, she came to realize the power of the written word. One of the best ways to help a child learn letter/sound connections is to give him lots of opportunities to write what he hears. He will begin with pictures, add letters, use "invented" spelling to construct words, and over time graduate to correct spelling.

> Learning to recognize letters and the sounds associated with letters is a vital step toward unlocking the meaning of written language.

Learning to recognize letters and the sounds associated with letters is a vital step toward unlocking the meaning of written language. Until a child breaks the phonics code, written words and letters are as mysterious as those Athens street signs were. Once the code is broken, a child gains access to written language *and* is able to get his message across.

Letter and sound recognition is important, but phonics by itself is not enough to comprehend and enjoy the written word. You must add the other ingredients in the reading mix.

Tips for Parents: Learning the Sounds Letters Make

- Teach your child the alphabet using alphabet songs and books. Play "I Spy": "I spy something that begins with the letter G."

- Encourage your child to write notes, make shopping lists, label drawings. Congratulate her on getting her message across. ("Do nt rek" is fine.)

- Read picture books with large letters and help your child hear the sounds the letters make by saying the beginning sound of a word and sliding a finger to the end as you blend the sounds.

- Play taped rhymes, chants, songs, poems, and stories and have your child "read" along.

- Point to a word and using prompts like "What sound do you think I'll hear at the beginning of this word? At the end?"

 Books That Help with Phonics

Picture Books

Dr. Seuss's ABC, Dr. Seuss

Q Is for Duck: An Alphabet Guessing Game, Mary Elting and Michael Folsom

Autumn: An Alphabet Acrostics, Steven Schnur

Cold Little Duck, Duck, Duck, Lisa Westberg Peters

Rain Talk, Mary Serfozo

Mortimer, Robert Munsch

The Aminal, Lorna Balian

Each Peach Pear Plum, Janet and Allan Ahlberg

Click, Clack, Moo: Cows That Type, Doreen Cronin

Chicka Chicka Boom Boom, Bill Martin

2. Word Knowledge (Lexical)

Even adult readers have difficulty with unfamiliar words. The first time you came upon a word such as *onomatopoeia*, you probably had to slow down and sound it out. Perhaps you pulled out the dictionary to confirm the pronunciation and to find out what it means. If the word *onomatopoeia* appeared several times in the same article, you would eventually be able to read it without slowing down at all. By the second or third time it appeared in the article, you wouldn't need to sound it out. You would have *word knowledge*.

Word knowledge is important because it is much faster than phonics. Think about a sentence like this: "Mother wants me to make my bed each morning." Now think about it like this: *"mmm, mmooo, th, moooth, eerr, wa, wa, wan, sts, sts, mmeee. . . ."* If you have to stop to sound out every syllable, it becomes cumbersome. By the time you're working on the fifth word, you've forgotten the first three and lost the stream of meaning. Of course, there's a time when children must sound out, but they need to move quickly to sight-reading. When a child can sight-read, it is often the moment when she takes off with reading. She recognizes and can pronounce many words, which increases her reading speed dramatically. All of a sudden, she's moving into longer books.

Word knowledge can begin when a child is still a toddler. When Chryse's son Carl was in preschool, he loved trucks. One particular book had pictures of every truck ever built. At his insistence, Chryse read that book to him hundreds of times. Carl began to identify and call out the words. He developed sight recognition of truck names. Likewise, when you plop your child in the shopping cart and push her through the grocery store, pointing to words like *milk, eggs, corn, diapers*, she learns to identify words found in daily life. She develops word knowledge.

Word knowledge is vital to reading fluently and well. Yet, like phonics, it alone is not enough. Recognizing words does not necessarily unlock the key to meaning. Think about reading Spanish: *¿Si todos los rios son dulces de dónde saca sal el mar?** You might need to sound out one or two of these words; the others, you can sight-read. But even if you can sight-read them, the sentence has no meaning if you don't know Spanish. That's what it's like for children when they're still operating at the surface level. They haven't yet added the "chocolate chips" of meaning.

---

*"If all rivers are sweet where does the sea get its salt?" *The Book of Questions*, Pablo Neruda.

Tips for Parents: Developing Word Knowledge

- Point out the writing that surrounds us on street signs, on billboards, in grocery stores

- Reread favorite books (as your child listens and follows the words, she builds her mental storehouse of sight words)

- Talk about how the same word can look different because of uppercase letters or different print styles (for example, bed, BED)

- Make labels for his environment (for example, DESK, CHAIR, DOOR, WALL, FLOOR)

- Use prompts like "Have you seen this word before?"

Books That Help Develop Word Knowledge

Picture Books

I Love Animals, Flora McDonnell

Whose Mouse Are You? Robert Kraus

Water Dance, Thomas Locker

Across the Stream, Mirra Ginsburg

Oh, A-Hunting We Will Go, John Langstaff

Don't Forget the Bacon, Pat Hutchins

My Brown Bear Barney, Dorothy Butler

Homeplace, Anne Shelby

When I Was Young in the Mountains, Cynthia Rylant

What a Wonderful Day to Be a Cow, Carolyn Lesser

3. Language Structure (Syntax)

Syntax is the way words are put together to form phrases or sentences. It is language's architecture. Punctuation and grammar are part of syntax. The meaning of words can vary a great deal depending on how they are laced together. For example, think of this unpunctuated sentence: "Woman without her man is nothing." Add a little punctuation: "Woman, without her man, is nothing." Let's punctuate it again: "Woman! Without her, man is nothing." A comma or two can completely change the meaning of a sentence. In many ways, syntax is the bridge between the surface and deep systems, because how words, phrases, and sentences are linked and punctuated greatly affects what they mean.

Children begin learning syntax from the time they are babies and hear and mimic the people around them. When, as preschoolers, Susan's children listened to her husband reading books like *The Hobbit* and *The Lion, the Witch, and the Wardrobe,* they were learning syntax. They heard words being strung together in complex sentences and paragraphs. They were learning how words built one upon the other to make stories. And they were learning what "sounds right."

Syntax is, in large part, auditory. You hear or read something and it sounds right, because your ear is attuned to the structure of the language. If someone said, "Pizza want I eat to," you wouldn't understand. If they said, "I want to eat pizza," you'd understand exactly. The way we sequence words, use grammar, and punctuate sentences has much to do with the meaning we get when we listen or read.

The more you hear how sentences flow, internalize how verbs typically follow nouns, linger over well-written phrases, talk with others, and read—or are read—good books, the better you understand and use syntax to create and clarify meaning.

Tips for Parents: Developing an Ear for Syntax

- Engage your child in conversation. Children *need* to hear themselves talk. They learn the shape and form of language by speaking and listening.

- Share wordless picture books and talk about what's happening in the pictures. Two suggestions are *Good Dog, Carl* by Alexandra Day and *Tuesday* by David Wiesner.

- Read a broad range of material to your child: picture books, chapter books, comics, poetry, and so on.

- Read books (picture books *and* longer books) with a lot of expression in your voice.

- Use prompts like "Did that sound right?"

 ### Books That Help with Syntax

Picture Books

Fireflies! Julie Brinckloe

Salt Hands, Jane Chelsea Aragon

Galimoto, Karen Lynn Williams

Roxaboxen, Barbara Cooney

Stellaluna, Janell Cannon

The Very Best of Friends, Margaret Wild

Yellow and Pink, William Steig

Longer Books

Tough Boy and Sister, Kirkpatrick Hill (121 pages)

Maniac Magee, Jerry Spinelli (184 pages)

When I Was Your Age: Volume Two, Amy Ehrlich (short stories; 187 pages)

INVISIBLE INGREDIENTS: DEEP STRUCTURES

Carpenters need certain tools to do their work. Without those tools, they can't build anything. With the tools—and with sturdy materials—they can construct strong, quality furniture. As important as having the right tools is the carpenter's willingness to use them. The more experience he has with using the tools, the easier it is for him to build, and the more beautiful his furniture becomes.

A reader also needs certain tools. The surface structure systems—phonics, word knowledge, and syntax—are indispensable. A reader has to have them to recognize and pronounce written language and needs to practice them to get good at deciphering language. But they

> Children entering school are not blank slates. In fact, they have already mastered oral language, a huge feat.

are far from enough to comprehend what is read. That requires development of the deep structure systems.

Children entering school are not blank slates. In fact, they have already mastered oral language, a huge feat. Children arrive at the school door with deep structure systems developed to varying degrees, depending on how much exposure they've had to language and how much language practice (talking and listening) they've had.

Already, they have life experience. They've been talking, listening, understanding, thinking, reasoning, manipulating their worlds, and often getting their way. That's the "material" they bring to school. As they learn the surface structure "tools" that allow them to decode written language, they are also learning to use the deep structure "tools," which allow them to design, measure, cut, assemble, screw, and glue the material into something real and meaningful. Building takes the material *plus* the tools *plus* learning to work with the tools and the materials. The wondrous thing your child is building is *meaning*.

4. Word Meanings/Associations (Semantics)

When Susan's daughter Alice was little, she'd go around the house singing, "The ants are my friends, they're blowin' in the wind" (*"The answer, my friends, is blowing in the wind"*—Bob Dylan). She'd heard the same thing that everyone else did but brought a totally different meaning to it.

Sometimes confusion arises because of different interpretations of the same words or phrases. There is good reason for that when you consider the complexities of English:

- The bandage was wound around the wound.

- The farm was used to produce produce.

- The dump was so full that it had to refuse more refuse.

- We must polish the Polish furniture.

- He could lead if he would get the lead out.

- The soldier decided to desert his dessert in the desert.

- I did not object to the object.

- The insurance was invalid for the invalid.

Word meanings are dependent upon their particular uses. The meanings of sentences derive from both the definitions of the individual words and *how* the words are used in a particular context.

Years ago, at Susan's husband's law firm, one of the junior partners had grown disenchanted with his work. The junior partner, Alan, went to an older partner and started his litany of complaints: "The work is boring. I don't like the clients. I hate my commute. It all feels so trivial."

Dan, the older partner, listened and asked Alan a question. "But what makes you really sore in your work?"

Alan launched in again: "My secretary drives me crazy. I'm tired of dealing with all the petty details. I don't enjoy—"

Dan stopped him. "Alan, listen, what makes you really sore in your work?"

"What?" Alan was puzzled.

Dan started flapping his arms. "Look, Alan, what makes you really *soar* in your work?"

"Ah." Alan smiled. "Now I get it. Well, you know, there *is* this one type of deal that I really love to put together. It's a great intellectual challenge. I've liked all the clients I've worked with on those transactions."

Alan ended up refocusing his practice so that he specialized in the one type of business deal that he thoroughly enjoyed. He has been wildly successful and much more fulfilled ever since—once he got the semantics right!

Tips for Parents: Developing a Good Understanding of Words

- Encourage your child to talk—better yet, joke—about what words mean in different contexts.

- Share how clues to a word's meaning can be found in the picture or the paragraph.

- Show how to make a best guess as to a word's meaning and then read ahead to find out if the guess was right.

- Have a box of old clothes, hats, and props your child can use to act out a favorite story.

- Start a parent–child book club. Your child can gain insight into the meaning of what was read by being a part of the discussion.

- Use prompts like "Does that word make sense?" and "What do you think this word means?"

Books Rich with Underlying Meaning

Picture Books

Creatures of Earth, Sea, and Sky, Georgia Heard (poetry)

Fly Away Home, Eve Bunting

See the Ocean, Estelle Condra

Twilight Comes Twice, Ralph Fletcher

The Stranger, Chris Van Allsburg

Amelia's Road, Linda Jacobs Altman

Longer Books

Amelia Bedelia, Peggy Parish (64 pages)

The Hundred Dresses, Eleanor Estes (80 pages)

Canyons, Gary Paulsen (184 pages)

The Giver, Lois Lowry (179 pages)

5. Background Knowledge (Schema)

At a teacher workshop in Green River, Wyoming, Susan put the following on the overhead projector:

K2 (P5, K2) across

P2 * K2 tog, YO, K1,YO

SSK, P2; repeat from * across

In unison, the teachers in the audience began chanting "Knit 2, pearl 5, knit 2. . . ." Susan has used that transparency all over the country. Usually, after a pause, mumbles, and confused looks, one or two people timidly raise their hands. "It's knitting instructions," they'll say. In Green River, the choral reading resulted from a high concentration of knitters. They knew exactly what the overhead meant, because of their background knowledge.

Background knowledge is basically all the life experience you bring to what you read. It is all that you've read, felt, heard, seen, tasted, smelled, touched, visited, and encountered.

If you reside on the Maine coast and sail, you read *Moby Dick* differently from those who live in Kansas. If you've never lived in the Rockies, you read Wallace Stegner's *Angle of Repose* differently from Coloradoans who spend time hiking, rafting, and backcountry skiing in Stegner's country. If you listen to Vivaldi's *Four Seasons*, you hear it differently if you are a violinist. The understanding you bring to a piece and the meaning you take from it vary according to your background knowledge. That is not to say that you need to spend time whaling to enjoy *Moby Dick* or need to be a violinist to appreciate Vivaldi. It *is* saying that you will read or listen differently depending upon your life experience.

In many ways, background knowledge is your life's connective tissue, linking your past with your present, giving texture and dimension to your relationships, your work, your pastimes, your thinking. It is vitally important in reading, because the printed word can be understood only by the *meaning* a reader brings to it. For children, activating and building background knowledge are critical to gaining meaning from reading.

Tips for Parents: Using and Developing Background Knowledge

- Provide experiences for your child. Picnics, museum outings, visits to the library, walks around the block are anchor experiences from which he can draw as a reader.

- Help your child follow her passions. If she's into frogs, snakes, fairy tales, rocks—whatever—get the books and read them to her.

- Talk with your child about his experiences and help him connect them to his reading or listening.

- Talk about your memories sparked by a book.

- Use prompts like "This is just like the time I . . ." "Doesn't this remind you of . . . ."

Books That Build Background Knowledge

Picture Books

Bats, Gail Gibbons

Follow the Drinking Gourd, Jeanette Winter

Up North at the Cabin, Marsha Wilson Chall

Walking the Log: Memories of a Southern Childhood, Bessie Nickens

So Far from the Sea, Eve Bunting

Coming Home: From the Life of Langston Hughes, Floyd Cooper

The King's Day, Aliki

Longer Books

Number the Stars, Lois Lowry (137 pages)

Catherine, Called Birdy, Karen Cushman (212 pages)

Roll of Thunder, Hear My Cry, Mildred C. Taylor (276 pages)

6. Knowledge of Audience/Purpose (Pragmatic)

Ten years ago, Susan's family took up river rafting. They bought a boat and all the gear that goes with it. Every January, they fill out applications and hope that by March they'll get a permit or two.

Once they know the rivers they'll be rafting, Susan goes to Down-River Expeditions and buys river guidebooks, which include detailed descriptions of the rivers with such information as geological formations and a snapshot of the flora and fauna and, most important, a mile-by-mile map of the river that shows where the rapids are located and that rates their difficulty. The geology and natural history are interesting, but she buys the guide for one reason: She wants to know exactly where the rapids are, which ones they need to pull over and scout before running, what the recommended route is, and what rocks and holes they need to avoid. Susan would never have bought a river guide if her family hadn't taken up rafting. She reads the books for the most pragmatic reason possible: She wants her family to make it down the river alive and unhurt.

There are many things that people read only for pragmatic purposes: a cookbook, a first-aid manual, instructions for games, a computer manual, travel guides, sewing patterns, car manuals. Suppose you're getting ready to make a presentation. You might read the material, make an outline, prepare PowerPoint slides, read the material again, then rehearse your presentation. Your purpose dictates the way you read. It is very different from blasting through that gripping novel you just can't put down.

The Harry Potter phenomenon demonstrates a different type of purposeful reading. Although many young readers are enchanted by the plots, they also long to be part of the "Harry Club." Their peers know the wizard ways of their hero, and they, too, want to know. Being part of this "in" group has a lot to do with their will to read. They want to be able to talk with friends and speculate about what's to come. They have a very pragmatic reason for reading the books. A side benefit is that this might be the first time they've experienced the addictive quality of a "good read." Their purpose for diving into

Harry Potter's adventures fuels their engagement in reading. They learn that it's fun!

In other words, part of reading is being aware of *why* you are reading. There are times when you just want to skim some material; other times when you want to master it; times when you read for pleasure; others when you read for work or school. The pragmatic system has to do with being aware of the purpose of your reading, and reading according to that purpose.

Tips for Parents: Thinking About the Reason for Reading

- Talk about all the reasons you read (for example, to play a board game, make a cake, plan a trip, put together a toy, fix a bike, have fun).

- Encourage your child to think about why he is reading: for fun, for information, to do a school assignment, to write a paper.

- Create specific reasons to read: to build a model airplane, find information on the Internet, make brownies, be part of a book group discussion.

- Use prompts like "I need to read this because . . . ."

Books to Discuss Together

Picture Books

Tight Times, Barbara Shook Hazen

Teammates, Peter Golenbock

The Lily Cupboard: A Story of the Holocaust, Shulamith Levey Oppenheim

Baseball Saved Us, Ken Mochizuke

Faithful Elephants, Yukio Tsuchiya

Smoky Night, Eve Bunting

The Wretched Stone, Chris Van Allsburg

Longer Books

Fig Pudding, Ralph Fletcher (136 pages)

Bridge to Terabithia, Katherine Paterson (128 pages)

Onion John, Joseph Krumgold (248 pages)

Ultimately, we read . . . to strengthen the self and to learn its authentic interests.

—Harold Bloom

Afterword

Everyone who knows how to read has it in their power to
magnify themselves, to multiply the ways in which they
exist to make their life full, significant, and interesting.

—ALDOUS HUXLEY

W E WANT YOUR child to be ravenous for reading. We want him to pick up a book and set out on a journey, feed an interest, explore a passion. We want him to realize that books are friends that connect him to people and ideas from across the globe and throughout the ages. We want your child to become not just a school reader but a lifetime reader who understands that reading is a free pass to entertainment, adventure, and a rich, productive life. If a child thinks reading is about skill sheets, workbooks, vocabulary lists, and test scores, he will never love to read. But if he sees you as a reader, as someone to share the reading journey with him, he will be ready to leap into this exciting, mind-expanding world.

The 7 Keys unlock your child's intellectual awareness, give her power over words, make her an active player in her own learning. They will help your child become entranced by stories, moved by historical and current events, and engaged in the world around her so that she is a better citizen, friend, and community member. Your child will become a mindful reader who can't wait to find out what happens next, who is stimulated by what she reads and wants to read more, who reads to gain new ideas and insights, who understands and appreciates the power of words, and who, ultimately, will live life more fully. It's about reading for meaning. It's about thinking. It's about comprehending to better remember and more deeply understand.

Now your child can read it and get it. May the 7 Keys unlock many new vistas and help build a rich connection of shared stories, interests, and love for you and your child!

Then one day, from the window of a car (the destination of that journey is now forgotten), I saw a billboard by the side of the road. The sight could not have lasted very long; perhaps the car stopped for a moment, perhaps it just slowed down long enough for me to see, large and looming, shapes similar to those in my book, but shapes that I had never seen before. And yet, all of a sudden, I knew what they were, I heard them in my head, they metamorphosed from black lines and white spaces into a solid, sonorous, meaningful reality. I had done this all by myself. No one had performed the magic for me. I and the shapes were alone together, revealing ourselves in a silently respectful dialogue. Since I could turn bare lines into living reality, I was all-powerful. I could read.

—Alberto Manguel

Bibliography

PROFESSIONAL LITERATURE

Galbraith, Judy. *You Know Your Child Is Gifted When . . . : A Beginner's Guide to Life on the Bright Side.* Minneapolis: Free Spirit Publishing, 2000.

Hart, Betty, and Todd R. Risley. *Meaningful Differences in the Everyday Experience of Young American Children.* Baltimore: Paul H. Brooks, 1995.

Harvey, Stephanie. *Nonfiction Matters: Reading, Writing, and Research in Grades 3–8.* Portland, Maine: Stenhouse, 1998.

Harvey, Stephanie, and Anne Goudvis. *Strategies That Work: Teaching Comprehension to Enhance Understanding.* Portland, Maine: Stenhouse, 2000.

Jensen, Eric. *Teaching with the Brain in Mind.* Alexandria, Va.: Association for Supervision & Curriculum Development, 1998.

Keene, Ellin Oliver, and Susan Zimmermann. *Mosaic of Thought: Teaching Comprehension in a Reader's Workshop.* Portsmouth, N.H.: Heinemann, 1997.

Miller, Debbie. *Reading with Meaning.* Portland, Maine: Stenhouse, 2002.

Pearson, P. D., L. R. Roehler, J. A. Dole, and G. G. Duffy. "Developing Expertise in Reading Comprehension." In J. Samuels and

A. Farstrup, eds., *What Research Has to Say About Reading Instruction*. Newark, Del.: International Reading Association, 1992.

Rumelhart, D. *Toward an Interactive Model of Reading* (Tech. Rep. No. 56). San Diego: University of California Center for Human Information Processing, 1976.

Sweeney, Diane. *Learning Along the Way: Professional Development by and for Teachers*. Portland, Maine: Stenhouse, 2003.

Tovani, Cris. *I Read It, But I Don't Get It: Comprehension Strategies for Adolescent Readers*. Portland, Maine: Stenhouse, 2000.

U.S. Department of Education. *How to Help Every Child Become a Reader*. CITY: Your Domain Publishing, 2001.

Wells, G. *Language, Learning, and Education*. Berkshire, England: Windsor, 1985.

BOOKS

Abercrombie, Barbara. *Charlie Anderson*. New York: Aladdin, 1995.

Adler, David A. *Lou Gehrig: The Luckiest Man*. San Diego: Harcourt Brace, 2001.

Ahlberg, Janet, and Allan Ahlberg. *Each Peach Pear Plum*. New York: Penguin USA, 1999.

Aliki. *The King's Day: Louis XIV of France*. New York: HarperCollins Juvenile Books, 1991.

Altman, Linda Jacobs. *Amelia's Road*. New York: Lee and Low, 1993.

Andrews, Jan. *Very Last First Time*. New York: Groundwood, 2003.

Aragon, Jane Chelsea. *Salt Hands*. New York: Puffin, 1994.

Avi. *Poppy*. New York: HarperCollins, 2001.

Babbitt, Natalie. *Tuck Everlasting*. New York: Farrar, Straus and Giroux, 1986.

Balian, Lorna. *The Aminal*. Shakopee, Minn: Humbug Books, 1994.

Ballard, Robert D. *Exploring the Titanic.* New York: Scholastic Paperbacks, 1998.

Barbalet, Margaret. *The Wolf.* New York: Macmillan, 1992.

Barron, T. A. *The Ancient One.* New York: Philomel Books, 1992.

Barron, T. A. *The Lost Years of Merlin.* New York: Philomel Books, 1996.

Brinckloe, Julie. *Fireflies!* New York: Aladdin Books, 1986.

Brown, Margaret Wise. *The Runaway Bunny.* New York: HarperFestival, 1991.

Brown, Margaret Wise. *The Important Book.* New York: Harper and Row, 1997.

Bunting, Eve. *Fly Away Home.* New York: Clarion Books, 1993.

Bunting, Eve. *A Day's Work.* New York: Houghton Mifflin, 1997.

Bunting, Eve. *So Far from the Sea.* New York: Clarion Books, 1998.

Bunting, Eve. *Smoky Night.* San Diego: Harcourt, 1999.

Butler, Dorothy. *My Brown Bear Barney.* New York: Greenwillow, 1989.

Cannon, Janell. *Stellaluna.* New York: Harcourt, 1993.

Cannon, Janell. *Verdi.* New York: Harcourt, 1997.

Chall, Marsha Wilson. *Up North at the Cabin.* New York: Lothrop Lee & Shepard, 1992.

Cleary, Beverly. *Dear Mr. Henshaw.* New York: HarperCollins, 2000.

Coerr, Eleanor. *Sadako and the Thousand Paper Cranes.* New York: Penguin Putnam, 1977.

Condra, Estelle. *See the Ocean.* Nashville, Tenn.: Eager Minds Press, 2002.

Cooney, Barbara. *Miss Rumphius.* New York: Viking, 1982.

Cooney, Barbara. *Roxaboxen.* New York: Scholastic, 1992.

Cooper, Floyd. *Coming Home: From the Life of Langston Hughes.* New York: Paper Star, 1998.

Creech, Sharon. *Walk Two Moons*. New York: HarperTrophy, 1996.

Crews, Donald. *Shortcut*. New York: Greenwillow, 1992.

Cronin, Doreen. *Click, Clack, Moo: Cows That Type*. New York: Simon and Schuster, 2000.

Cushman, Karen. *Catherine, Called Birdy*. New York: HarperTrophy, 1995.

Dahl, Roald. *Matilda*. New York: Puffin, 1998.

Day, Alexandra. *Good Dog, Carl*. New York: Little Simon, 1996.

DeFelice, Cynthia C. *When Grampa Kissed His Elbow*. New York: Macmillan, 1992.

DiCamillo, Kate. *Because of Winn-Dixie*. Cambridge, Mass.: Candlewick Press, 2001.

Dorros, Arthur. *Abuela*. New York: Dutton, 1997.

Dr. Seuss. *Dr. Seuss's ABC: An Amazing Book*. New York: Random House, 1996.

Dragonwagon, Crescent. *Home Place*. New York: Macmillan, 1999.

Ehlert, Lois. *Red Leaf, Yellow Leaf*. New York: Harcourt Brace, 1991.

Ehrlich, Amy. (Ed). *When I Was Your Age: Volume Two*. Cambridge, Mass.: Candlewick Press, 2002.

Elting, Mary, and Michael Folsom. *Q Is for Duck: An Alphabet Guessing Game*. Boston: Houghton Mifflin, 1985.

Estes, Eleanor. *The Hundred Dresses*. San Diego: Harcourt Brace, 1988.

Falconer, Ian. *Olivia Saves the Circus*. New York: Atheneum, 2001.

Fleischman, Paul. *Bull Run*. New York: Harper Trophy, 1993.

Fleischman, Sid. *The Whipping Boy*. New York: Troll Communication, 1987.

Fletcher, Ralph. *Fig Pudding*. New York: Yearling Books, 1996.

Fletcher, Ralph. *Twilight Comes Twice*. New York: Houghton Mifflin, 1997.

Foreman, Michael. *War Boy*. New York: Arcade Publishing, 2000.

Fox, Mem. *Koala Lou*. San Diego: Harcourt Brace, 1994.

Fox, Paula. *The Slave Dancer*. New York: Yearling, 1996.

Fritz, Jean. *What's the Big Idea, Ben Franklin*. New York: Penguin Putnam, 1996.

Garland, Sherry. *The Lotus Seed*. San Diego: Harcourt, 1993.

George, Jean Craighead. *Julie of the Wolves*. New York: HarperTrophy, 1974.

Gerstein, Mordicai. *The Seal Mother*. New York: E. P. Dutton, 1987.

Gibbons, Gail. *Monarch Butterfly*. New York: Holiday House, 1991.

Gibbons, Gail. *Bats*. New York: Holiday House, 2000.

Ginsburg, Mirra. *Across the Stream*. New York: Mulberry Books, 1991.

Golding, William. *Lord of the Flies*. New York: Penguin Putnam, 1959.

Golenbock, Peter. *Teammates*. San Diego: Harcourt Brace, 1992.

Graves, Donald. *Baseball, Snakes, and Summer Squash: Poems About Growing Up*. Honesdale, Pa.: Boyds Mills, 1996.

Greenfield, Eloise. *Under the Sunday Tree*. New York: HarperCollins Children's Books, 1988.

Hakin, Joy. *A History of U.S.* New York: Oxford University Press Children's Books, 2002.

Hammarskjöld, Dag. *Markings*. New York: Alfred A. Knopf, 1971.

Hawes, Judy. *Fireflies in the Night*. New York: Harper Collins, 1991.

Hazen, Barbara Shook. *Tight Times*. New York: Viking, 1983.

Heard, Georgia. *Creatures of Earth, Sea, and Sky: Poems*. Honesdale, Pa.: Boyds Mills, 1997.

Heide, Florence Parry, and J. D. Gilliland. *The Day of Ahmed's Secret.* New York: Lothrop, Lee and Shepard, 1990.

Henkes, Kevin. *Chrysanthemum.* New York: Mulberry Books, 1996.

Hesse, Karen. *Out of the Dust.* New York: Scholastic Paperbacks, 1999.

Hewett, Joan. *Rosalie.* New York: Lothrop, Lee and Shepard, 1987.

Hill, Kirkpatrick. *Toughboy and Sister.* New York: Penguin Putnam, 2001.

Hoffman, Mary. *Amazing Grace.* New York: Dial Books for Young Readers, 1991.

Holt, Kimberly Willis. *My Louisiana Sky.* New York: Henry Holt and Co, 1998.

Honda, Tetsuya. *Wild Horse Winter.* San Francisco: Chronicle, 1995.

Hutchins, Pat. *Don't Forget the Bacon.* New York: HarperTrophy, 1994.

Innocenti, Roberto. *Rose Blanche.* New York: Harcourt, 1996.

Janeczko, Paul B. (Ed.). *The Place My Words Are Looking For.* New York: Bradbury, 1990.

Khalsa, Dayal Kaur. *Tales of a Gambling Grandma.* Toronto: Tundra Books, 1994.

Killilea, Marie. *Newf.* New York: Philomel, 1996.

Kiser, SuAnn, and Kevin Kiser. *The Birthday Thing.* New York: Greenwillow, 1989.

Kitchen, Bert. *And So They Build.* Cambridge, Mass.: Candlewick Press, 1993.

Konigsburg, E. L. *From the Mixed-Up Files of Mrs. Basil E. Frankweiler.* New York: Aladdin, 1998.

Kramer, Stephen. *Avalanche.* Minneapolis: Carolrhoda Books, 1992.

Kraus, Robert. *Whose Mouse Are You?* New York: Aladdin, 1986.

Kroll, Steven. *Lewis and Clark: Explorers of the American West*. New York: Holiday House, 1996.

Krumgold, Joseph. *Onion John*. New York: HarperTrophy, 1984.

L'Engle, Madeleine. *A Wrinkle in Time*. New York: Yearling, 1973.

Lahiri, Jhumpa. *Interpreter of Maladies*. Boston: Houghton Mifflin, 1999.

LaMarche, Jim. *The Raft*. New York: HarperTrophy, 2002.

Langstaff, John. *Oh, A-Hunting We Will Go*. New York: Simon and Schuster, 1991.

Lawson, Robert. *Ben and Me: A New and Astonishing Life of Benjamin Franklin as Written by His Good Mouse Amos*. New York: Little Brown, 1988.

Lesser, Carolyn. *What a Wonderful Day to Be a Cow*. New York: Knopf, 1995.

Levine, Gail Carson. *Ella Enchanted*. New York: HarperTrophy, 1998.

Lewis, C. S. *The Lion, the Witch, and the Wardrobe*. New York: Harper-Collins Juvenile Books, 2000.

Lewis, Kim. *Floss*. Cambridge, Mass.: Candlewick Press, 1994.

Lobel, Arnold. *Frog and Toad Together*. New York: HarperTrophy, 1979.

Locker, Thomas. *Water Dance*. New York: Harcourt Brace, 1997.

Lowry, Lois. *The Giver*. New York: Random House, 2002.

MacLachlan, Patricia. *Sarah, Plain and Tall*. New York: Harper-Trophy, 1987.

MacLachlan, Patricia. *The Sick Day*. New York: Random House, 2003.

Martin, Bill. *Chicka Chicka Boom Boom*. New York: Simon and Schuster, 1989.

Martin, C. L. G. *Three Brave Women*. New York: Macmillan, 1991.

Mazer, Harry. *A Boy at War: A Novel of Pearl Harbor.* New York: Simon and Schuster, 2002.

McBride, James. *The Color of Water.* New York: Riverhead Books, 1996.

McCully, Emily Arnold. *Four Hungry Kittens.* New York: Penguin Putnam, 2001.

McDonnell, Flora. *I Love Animals.* Cambridge, Mass.: Candlewick Press, 2001.

McKee, David. *Elmer.* New York: Lothrop Lee & Shepard, 1989.

Mitchell, Margaree King. *Uncle Jed's Barbershop.* New York: Simon and Schuster, 1998.

Mochizuke, Ken. *Baseball Saved Us.* New York: Lee & Low, 1995.

Mochizuki, Ken. *Passage to Freedom: The Sugihara Story.* New York: Lee & Low, 1997.

Moss, Marissa. *Regina's Big Mistake.* Boston: Houghton Mifflin, 1995.

Moss, Marissa. *Rachel's Journal.* San Diego: Harcourt Brace, 1998.

Munsch, Robert. *Mortimer.* Toronto: Annick Press, 1985.

Munsch, Robert. *The Paper Bag Princess.* Toronto: Annick Press, 1988.

Nelson, Sharlene, and Ted Nelson. *Mount St. Helens National Volcanic Monument.* New York: Children's Press, 1997.

Nickens, Bessie. *Walking the Log: Memories of a Southern Childhood.* New York: Rizzoli, 1994.

Oppenheim, Shulamith Levey. *The Lily Cupboard: A Story of the Holocaust.* New York: HarperTrophy, 1992.

Parish, Peggy. *Amelia Bedelia.* New York: HarperCollins, 1992.

Park, Frances, and Ginger Park. *The Royal Bee.* Honesdale, Pa.: Boyds Mills, 2000.

Paterson, Katherine. *Bridge to Terabithia.* New York: HarperTrophy, 1987.

Paulsen, Gary. *My Life in Dog Years*. New York: Bantam Doubleday Dell, 1988.

Paulsen, Gary. *Canyons*. New York: Bantam Doubleday Dell, 1991.

Paulsen, Gary. *The Tortilla Factory*. San Diego: Harcourt Brace, 1998.

Paulsen, Gary. *Hatchet*. New York: Pocket Books, 1999.

Peet, Bill. *The Pinkish, Purplish, Bluish Egg*. Boston: Houghton Mifflin, 1984.

Peters, Lisa Westberg. *Cold Little Duck, Duck, Duck*. New York: HarperCollins, 2000.

Polacco, Patricia. *Thunder Cake*. New York: Philomel, 1990.

Polacco, Patricia. *Pink and Say*. New York: Philomel, 1994.

Pollan, Michael. *The Botany of Desire: A Plant's-Eye View of the World*. New York: Random House, 2001.

Reiss, Johanna. *The Upstairs Room*. New York: HarperTrophy, 1990.

Ringgold, Faith. *Tar Beach*. New York: Crown, 1991.

Rylant, Cynthia. *Missing May*. New York: Bantam Doubleday Dell, 1993.

Rylant, Cynthia. *When I Was Young in the Mountains*. New York: E. P. Dutton, 1993.

Rylant, Cynthia. *The Van Gogh Cafe*. New York: Scholastic, 1995.

Rylant, Cynthia. *An Angel for Solomon Singer*. New York: Orchard, 1996.

Sachar, Louis. *Holes*. New York: Yearling, 2000.

Sakai, Kimiko. *Sachiko Means Happiness*. San Francisco: Children's Book Press, 1990.

Sandburg, Carl. *Carl Sandburg Selected Poems*. New York: Gramercy Books, 1992.

Sandburg, Carl. *Grassroots*. San Diego: Harcourt Brace, 1998.

Santella, Andrew. *Lewis and Clark*. New York: Franklin Watts, 2002.

Say, Allen. *A River Dream*. Boston: Houghton Mifflin, 1993.

Say, Allen. *El Chino*. Boston: Houghton Mifflin, 1996.

Say, Allen. *The Sign Painter*. Boston: Houghton Mifflin, 2000.

Schnur, Steven. *Autumn: An Alphabet Acrostic*. New York: Clarion, 1997.

Serfozo, Mary. *Rain Talk*. New York: Macmillan, 1990.

Shelby, Anne. *Homeplace*. New York: Scholastic, 2000.

Simon, Seymour. *Animals Nobody Loves*. New York: SeaStar Books, 2001.

Sobol, Donald J. *Two-Minute Mysteries*. New York: Scholastic, 1991.

Soto, Gary. *Neighborhood Odes*. San Diego: Harcourt Brace, 1992.

Spinelli, Jerry. *Maniac Magee*. Boston: Little, Brown and Company, 1990.

Steig, William. *Yellow and Pink*. New York: Farrar, Straus and Giroux, 1984.

Taylor, Mildred C. *Roll of Thunder, Hear My Cry*. New York: Puffin, 1997.

Tolkein, J. R. R. *The Hobbit*. Boston: Houghton Mifflin, 2002.

Tsuchiya, Yukio. *Faithful Elephants: A True Story of Animals, People, and War*. Boston: Houghton Mifflin, 1997.

Uchida, Yoshiko. *The Bracelet*. New York: Philomel Books, 1996.

Upton, Pat. *Who Does This Job?* Honesdale, Pa.: Boyds Mills, 1991.

Van Allsburg, Chris. *The Stranger*. Boston: Houghton Mifflin, 1986.

Van Allsburg, Chris. *Two Bad Ants*. Boston: Houghton Mifflin, 1988.

Van Allsburg, Chris. *The Wretched Stone*. Boston: Houghton Mifflin, 1991.

Viorst, Judith. *The Tenth Good Thing About Barney*. New York: Simon and Schuster, 1971.

Whelan, Gloria. *Homeless Bird*. New York: HarperTrophy, 2001.

Wiesner, David. *Tuesday*. New York: Clarion, 1991.

Wild, Margaret. *The Very Best of Friends*. San Diego: Voyager, 1994.

Wild, Margaret. *Let the Celebrations Begin!* New York: Orchard, 1996.

Williams, Karen Lynn. *Galimoto*. New York: Mulberry Books, 1991.

Winter, Jeanette. *Follow the Drinking Gourd*. New York: Trumpet, 1988.

Woodson, Jacqueline. *The Other Side*. New York: Putnam, 2001.

Worth, Valerie. *All the Small Poems*. New York: Farrar, Straus, and Giroux, 1987.

Yolen, Jane. *Owl Moon*. New York: Philomel, 1987.

Yolen, Jane. *Encounter*. San Diego: Harcourt Brace, 1992.

Index

About the Authors

Susan Zimmermann is the coauthor of *Mosaic of Thought: Teaching Comprehension in a Reader's Workshop* (1997), an educational bestseller that is changing the way reading is taught in classrooms throughout America. She cofounded and served as the Executive Director of the Denver-based Public Education and Business Coalition where she initiated the Reading Project. A Yale Law School graduate, she is also the author of *Writing to Heal the Soul* (2002), and *Grief Dancers* (1996). Noted speaker and workshop leader, Susan works with school districts and organizations throughout the United States on ways to deepen reading and writing experiences for adults and children. She lives in the foothills west of Denver with her husband, Paul Phillips, and their four children.

Chryse Hutchins has been a classroom teacher, staff developer, and adjunct Professor of Literacy at the University of Denver. For the past 14 years, she has worked with the Denver-based Public Education and Business Coalition, providing on-site training to classroom teachers in reading and writing instruction. A literacy consultant, she works with educators across the country and internationally, speaking at conferences, providing demonstration lessons, facilitating school-wide comprehension implementation plans, and presenting at parent nights. A mother of two, Chryse lives in Denver with her husband, Steve.